Daffodil and Tulip Yearbook 1999-2000

*An annual for amateurs and specialists
growing and showing
daffodils, snowdrops and tulips*

in association with

The Royal Horticultural Society

LONDON

Published in 1999 by
The Royal Horticultural Society,
80 Vincent square, London SW1P 2PE

All rights reserved. No part of this publication may be reproduced in any form or by any means, without permission from the Publisher

ISBN 1-874431-96-5
© The Royal Horticultural Society 1999

EDITORIAL COMMITTEE

M S Bradbury (*Honorary Editor*)

Mrs W M Akers

J L Akers

J W Blanchard

J Dalton

A J R Pearson

B S Duncan

D J Pearce

Lady Skelmersdale

Opinions expressed by the authors are not necessarily those of the Royal Horticultural Society

Printed by the KPC Group London & Ashford Kent

Contents

ILLUSTRATIONS 5

EDITORIAL 6

MINIATURE DAFFODILS FROM
DIVISIONS 1 - 4 by *Delia Bankhead* 7

MORE AGM DAFFODILS AND TULIPS
Wisley Daffodil Trials 1999
by *David Matthews* 11
AGM Tulips
by *James L Akers* 12

CYCLAMINEUS HYBRIDS IN THE
GARDEN by *Christine Skelmersdale* 13

CARLO ALBERTO NAEF - "THE
GUV'NOR" by *Jan Dalton* 15

GROWING SNOWDROPS
by *John Grimshaw* 17

N. CYCLAMINEUS AND ITS HYBRIDS -
A SYMPOSIUM 20
Breeding Activity and Problems
by *Malcolm Bradbury* 20
N. cyclamineus in the Wild
by *Malcolm Bradbury* 22
The English Contribution
by *Malcolm Bradbury* 23
Division 6 from Ireland
by *Janine Doulton* 24
American Bred Cyclamineus Cultivars
by *Delia Bankhead* 26
Tracing Trena Territory in New Zealand
by *David Adams* 28
Cyclamineus Hybrids in Australia
by *Richard Perrignon* 30
The Miniature Cyclamineus Cultivars
by *Delia Bankhead* 30

Judging Cyclamineus Hybrids
by *John Blanchard* 33

FOUR DECADES ON
by *Frank Verge* 35

BREEDING ENGLISH FLORISTS'
TULIPS
by *John Wainwright* 36

DAFFODILS AND TULIPS IN LATVIA
by *Malcolm Bradbury* 38

NEW CHROMOSOME COUNTS IN
NARCISSUS CULTIVARS
by *Peter Brandham* 39

A SECOND VISIT TO THE HORTUS
BULBORUM by *Wendy Akers* 45

OBITUARY; ALAN HARDY VMH
by *Fred Whitsey* 46

DAFFODIL AND TULIP NOTES 47
"Thomas' Virescent Daffodil", syn. The
Derwydd Daffodil by *Sally Kington* 47
Narcissus x christopheri = N. x koshinomurae
by *John Blanchard* 48
What a Delightful Flower
by *John and Elaine Ingamells* 48
World Daffodil Council
by *Bob Spotts* 49
The Ralph B White Memorial Medal 1999
by *Malcolm Bradbury* 50
Daffodils are Poisonous
by *Malcolm Bradbury* 50
The Peter Barr Memorial Cup Awarded
to James S Wells
by *Brian Duncan* 51
'White Owl' by *Sally Kington* 52

Madam Speaker
by Malcolm Bradbury   52

BOOK REVIEWS   53
AGS Bulb Issue *by Malcolm Bradbury*   53
Galanthus Gala 1998 *by Alan Leslie*   53
The Tulip *by James Akers*   54

OVERSEAS SHOWS AND NEWS   57
Pittsburgh Someplace Special
by Tony James   57
Australian Daffodil Season 1998
 by Richard Perrignon   58
New Zealand National Shows 1998   59

RHS SHOW DATES 2000   61

SNOWDROPS AT WESTMINSTER
by Alan Leslie   63
RHS EARLY DAFFODIL
COMPETITION
by John Goddard   65
RESULTS
by Peter Wilkins   65
RHS DAFFODIL SHOW
by Len Olive   67
RESULTS
by Peter Wilkins   69
RHS LATE DAFFODIL
COMPETITION
by Reg Nicholl   73

RESULTS
by Peter Wilkins   74
RHS TULIP COMPETITION
by James L Akers   77
RESULTS
by James L Akers   77

OTHER SHOWS   79
The Daffodil Society Show
by Jim Pearce   79
Tulips At Alpine Garden Society
Shows *by Alan Edwards*   81
Wakefield and North of England
Tulip Society
by Richard Smales   82
Daffodils and Tulips at Harrogate
by Richard Smales   83
South East England Daffodil Group
Show
by David Matthews   85
City of Belfast Show
by Wendy Akers   87

AWARDS TO DAFFODILS,
SNOWDROPS AND TULIPS   88

DAFFODIL AND TULIP COMMITTEE
1999   91

INDEX   93

Illustrations

Front cover
    Narcissus 'Garden Party' Best Bloom at the RHS Late Daffodil Competition. (Photos Great Britain)

page 14 Carlo Alberto Naef at his office desk shortly after his 90th birthday (J & E Page & Co Ltd)

page 19 "The home of Narcissus Ajax Cyclamineus" (Drawing taken from the front cover *Barr's Daffodils 1887*)

page 46 The late Alan Hardy, with favourite terrier in his garden at Sandling Park in front of *Pinus radiata* (from original introduction!) (The British Tourist Authority)

between pages 48 and 49

Fig. 1 *Narcissus* seedling 1-29-86 Best Bloom at the RHS Show. (Photos Great Britain)

Fig. 2 *Narcissus aureus* Best Miniature at the RHS Early Daffodil Competition. (Photos Great Britain)

Fig. 3 A vase of nine stems of *Tulipa* 'Prinses Irene' which won the Walter Blom Trophy at the RHS Tulip Competition. (Photos Great Britain)

Fig. 4 *Narcissus* seedling UU2611. (Richard and Elise Havens)

Fig. 5 *Narcissus* 'Crofty'. (Ron Scamp)

Fig. 6 *Narcissus* 'Itzim'. (Christine Skelmersdale)

Fig. 7 *Narcissus* 'Jack Snipe' (Christine Skelmersdale)

Fig. 8 *Narcissus* 'Noss Mayo' (Christine Skelmersdale)

Fig. 9 *Narcissus* 'Rapture' (Ron Scamp)

Fig. 10 *Narcissus* 'Andalusia' (Ron Scamp)

Fig. 11 *Narcissus* 'Trena' Best Bloom at the RHS Early Daffodil Competition. (Photos Great Britain)

Fig. 12 *Narcissus* 'Fiona MacKillop' (Reg Nicholl)

Fig. 13 Some members of the Daffodil and Tulip Trials Sub Committee during their visit to the Netherlands. (David Matthews)

Fig. 14 A drift of snowdrops at Hodsock Priory near Worksop. (Malcolm Bradbury)

Fig. 15 *Narcissus* 'My Angel'. (Jānis Rukšans)

Fig. 16 *Narcissus* "Thomas' Virescent Daffodil" (Sally Kington)

Fig. 17 Frost damage to daffodils (Malcolm Bradbury)

Fig. 18 Jānis Rukšans with his daffodils (Malcolm Bradbury)

Fig. 19 *Tulipa* 'Girlfriend'. (Malcolm Bradbury)

Fig. 20 *Tulipa* 'Golden Oxford', 'Pink Impression' and 'Olympic Flame'; Derek Williams' winning entry for the inaugural Tulip Championship of Great Britain at Harrogate Spring Show (James Akers)

Fig. 21 *Tulipa* 'Barcelona'. (James Akers)

Fig. 22 *Tulipa hageri splendens*. (James Akers)

Fig. 23 James (Jim) Wells (Jim Wells)

Fig. 24 Brian Duncan presenting the Bowles Challenge Cup to Eddie Jarman (Reg Nicholl)

Fig. 25 The Rt Hon Betty Boothroyd MP Speaker of the House of Commons, holding a bunch of *Narcissus* 'Madam Speaker' and talking to Ron Scamp. (Marie Curie Cancer Care)

Back cover
    The Gold Medal winning joint daffodil trade stand at the RHS Show (Photos Great Britain)

Editorial

The current edition of the *Yearbook* is the last of the Millennium. First published in 1913 the *Yearbook* and its readers have reflected our changing world. Early readers mostly employed gardeners to look after their very expensive bulbs, enjoyed large gardens and lived in Great Britain. Today, readers mostly look after their own much smaller gardens, pay significantly lower real prices for their bulbs and live world wide. Similarly, gardening is an optional peacetime activity and the fact that this is not the 87th edition of the *Yearbook* reflects both the disruptions caused by two World Wars and the time taken for leisure activities to recover from them.

A lasting change of direction was made as early as the second edition of the *Yearbook* in 1914. The "Preparatory Notice" announced that:

> "A feature which will commend itself to all is the inclusion of papers and notices from Australia, New Zealand, Holland and the United States - and this feature we hope may be extended and amplified in future issues, as it is evident that the interest in Daffodils is increasing in those distant lands."

In an age accustomed to Internet messages, telephone calls, air travel and regular World Conventions, the lands in question are thankfully no longer "distant". A fact we have sought to reflect both by appealing to a global readership and by seeking contributions from knowledgeable contributors world wide.

Recently the *Yearbook* has reflected the growing popularity of tulips and snowdrops by restoring the subsidiary coverage which had ended in 1971. As with daffodils, the aim is to continue publishing articles which are readable, interesting, authoritative and help to spread news and new developments quickly.

Sadly, this edition of the *Yearbook* records the passing of Alan Hardy VMH. Alan, whose wide range of horticultural interests extended well beyond daffodils, was a keen supporter and good friend of this publication. We extend our deepest sympathy to his widow Carolyn.

Readers will notice the temporary absence this year of two regular features. For the first time in many years John Blanchard has not recorded his latest trip to look at wild daffodils. This reflects John's conclusion that he saw nothing noteworthy. Second, this year, the Daffodil and Tulip Committee made no awards to daffodils for exhibition purposes. Such awards are helpful to exhibitors but can only be made if flowers are presented to the Committee for consideration. Hopefully, raisers and exhibitors will rise to the occasion and not let these important awards fall into disuse. Note, contributions by David Matthews and James Akers highlight the growth of Award of Garden Merit given to daffodils and tulips.

Gardeners will also find much of interest in Christine Skelmersdale's note on "Cyclamineus Hybrids in the Garden" and John Grimshaw's article on "Growing Snowdrops". Articles by Peter Brandham, Frank Verge and John Wainwright offer information about new chromosome counts for daffodils, successfully breeding daffodils on a small scale and unlocking the hidden breeding potential of English Florists' tulips. Following his article last year about daffodils at Alpine Garden Society Shows, Alan Edwards focuses on tulips this year. A non-competitive show perspective is provided by Alan Leslie's report on "Snowdrops at Westminster".

I am grateful to James and Wendy Akers for the many hours they have spent preparing camera ready copy for the printers. I would also like to thank the many contributors of the varied and interesting articles and pictures.

Malcolm Bradbury

Miniature Daffodils from Divisions 1-4

Delia Bankhead

The division 5 miniatures having been surveyed last year, this is a "catch-up" effort to bring the annual surveys of miniature cultivars into line with those of the standard daffodils. If the miniatures are the step-children of the daffodil world, surely those in the first four divisions rank somewhat below Cinderella in the attention that has been paid them by breeders. Of the 180 registered daffodil cultivars recognised as miniatures by the American Daffodil Society, only 55 fall into the first four divisions. Unlike their brethren amongst standard daffodils, nearly all were bred long ago.

All-Yellow Trumpets.
There are 33 trumpets, and nearly half are self yellows. The look-alike trio of 'Bagatelle', 'Little Gem' and 'Wee Bee' is almost too well-known to describe, except that they are the most commonly exhibited yellow trumpets. If my stocks are correctly named (and they agree with those I have seen elsewhere in the USA) there is nothing to distinguish between them. All are small mid-yellow flowers on short stems, with hooded perianths and slightly deeper yellow trumpets. Mr. Gerritsen also registered 'Petit Beurre', 'Piccolo' and 'Minidaf' in this colour code, but only 'Petit Beurre' is often seen. It is larger and taller than the three above, with a paler perianth. I have only just acquired 'Piccolo', which will bloom for the first time this year, and I believe 'Minidaf' has disappeared. According to a knowledgeable Dutch source, the only Dutch miniatures currently being grown in Holland are 'Bagatelle', 'Little Gem', 'Wee Bee', 'Little Beauty' and 'Rockery White'. He says all other stocks of Gerritsen miniatures have been discarded.

Alec Gray's contributions to the yellow trumpets are 'Charles Warren', another larger flower with a pale perianth rather similar to 'Petit Beurre', 'Gambas', 'Tanagra', and 'Skelmersdale Gold' (registered by Broadleigh Gardens, which I have seen only in photographs). 'Gambas' is a delightful little flower - very dwarf and quite small, with a trumpet having a lovely waisted form and a nice roll at the mouth. 'Tanagra' is slightly taller and later than the popular Dutch trio, and has better form, but is in the same general style, even to the hooded perianth. However this perianth is easier to flatten than the others. There is an unregistered flower of mysterious antecedents (no published data, except the date, 1978) that blooms very early, along with 'Gambas', and is the same size. 'Likely Lad' has a widely flaring trumpet that is really too large for the tiny perianth, but it is an appealing little flower, and a good grower.

Grant Mitsch's 'Small Talk', is quite distinctive, a deeper gold than most, and has more substance. It has a smooth but rather starry perianth, which sometimes has a deformed petal, but for all that, is a regular show winner. It is the last of the yellow trumpets to bloom in my garden. Mary Lou Gripshover's new 'Wyandot' is bred from 'Small Talk' and is a definite improvement, with a much better perianth. Matthew Fowld's 'Tiny Tot' is rarely seen and may have disappeared from gardens. The last two of this group are selected forms of species; 'Midget', a rather large, ungainly flower selected from *N. nanus*, and 'Douglasbank' from *N. minor*, which I have not seen.

Bicoloured Trumpets.
There are five trumpets coded as bicolours and two as reversed bicolours. The two old

Gerritsen W-Y registrations, 'Little Beauty' and 'Lilliput' are regularly seen on the show bench but leave much to be desired in terms of good form, and colour contrast. Both are rather large, and not particularly graceful. An American introduction of Murray Evans is 'Arrival', bred from 'Little Beauty', open pollinated. It is a smaller plant and flower, with slightly better form than its parent, but is pale and has hardly any contrast when it matures. None of these three has much substance. Alec Gray's 'Rupert' and 'Tosca' are the best of the bicolours. 'Tosca' is the more colourful, with a well formed, bright yellow trumpet and very white, but narrow petals. Its starry perianth is smooth, and has good substance. 'Rupert' is a different style, with a paler, more tubular trumpet and a broader, well overlapped perianth. If it were a more vigorous grower, it would be my choice for breeding. It has never set seed for me, but perhaps that is because it always seems to open during a very cold spell. I have just managed to replace 'Tosca' after a number of years without it, and do not know if it is fertile, but it should be.

Reversed Bicolour Trumpets.
'Gipsy Queen', 1YYW-WWY, is very prolific and fertile, and has a long record on the show bench, though it is not a great show flower. However, it is great in the garden and has produced some promising offspring (some in division 6). 'Sir Echo', the other reverse, is hardly one at all. It is another large miniature on a short stem that opens W-Y, and very slowly reverses to an extremely pale Y-W. It is not particularly vigorous and increases very slowly.

All-White Trumpets.
The whites are my favourite trumpets, and I grow all but 'Snug', which I believe is extinct. The two Dutch whites, 'Rockery White' and 'Rockery Gem', are not worth growing, as they never bloom. 'Rockery White' is still exported, and I have three different stocks of it, but in the many years I have had it, I have not seen one bloom. 'Rockery Gem' is all but extinct, and my small stock does not increase, or bloom. 'W. P. Milner', an old Backhouse introduction, is a charming flower much like *N. alpestris,* but not so white. It is not a show flower, but a clump is wonderful in the rock garden. 'Pledge', an unregistered flower of Michael Jefferson-Brown's, is the largest of the white trumpets; sometimes over 50mm (2in) in diameter and not as white as some. The perianth is very pointed and the petals sometimes twist. I have not tried to use it for breeding.

Alec Gray's whites are the ones to grow, show and use for breeding. The odd thing is, that not one of the five cultivars attributed to him was registered by Mr. Gray. One was registered by Michael Jefferson-Brown ('Candlepower'), two by Elizabeth Capen ('Alec Gray' and 'Elka'), one by myself ('Camborne') and 'Sprite' is unregistered. 'Elka' is the weakest, as it is a very shy bloomer, and requires regular, and fairly heavy feeding to make it bloom. It has a pointed, rather pinwheely perianth and not a lot of substance and 'Elka' is not so white as the others. However; it is a strong grower, and makes many offsets, but is reputedly a poor seeder. 'Alec Gray' and 'Candlepower' are the best - they are about equal in size and are somewhat smaller than the rest. Both have rather narrow petals, those on 'Alec Gray' being somewhat pointed, and on 'Candlepower' a little more blunt. 'Candlepower' has a slender trumpet which does not expand much and has a tight frill at the mouth. 'Alec Gray' has a slender, slightly expanding trumpet that is the longest of all five in proportion to the perianth, and has a nice roll at the end. Both open with a pale yellow trumpet which goes white in a day or two. 'Candlepower' is the more vigorous, and has a slight edge on substance, and both are very smooth. 'Sprite' is very similar to 'Alec Gray' in form, but is slightly larger, not so white, and not quite so refined. It has been a good grower for me. The last is a Gray seedling of unknown parentage registered as 'Camborne' in 1995. It was discovered in a stock of 'Tosca' by Kate Reade, who had received the bulbs from Mr. Gray. She kindly shared it with me, subsequently lost her stock, and even more kindly allowed me to register it. I did so because it is unlike any other miniature white trumpet, having wide ace-of-spades petals and an overlapping double triangle perianth. It also has a ruffled and evenly rolled trumpet, which sometimes nicks the petals. It is a little shy on substance, and can be rather ribby, but on the whole, is a good flower and a very strong grower. Order of bloom for the five is: 'Camborne', 'Candlepower', 'Alec Gray', 'Sprite' and 'Elka'. The first four all have good seed and pollen. I have not tried 'Elka', but because it blooms later than the rest, perhaps it could be used to extend the season for white trumpets.

Division 2.
The eleven cultivars in division 2 are a motley bunch with little in common. Rather than by colour, these will be assessed roughly by size - a group of larger ones, then a group of tiny ones. 'Marionette', 2Y-YYO, is a bit of a freak, having one of the largest flowers (intermediate size) on the entire list, but a very short stem, barely 10cm (4in) tall. 'Mustardseed', (Gray) and 'Picarillo' (Mulligan) are two average size 2Y-Ys. Neither is very good. 'Mustardseed' is a good grower, but has very poor form, with gappy, lozenge shaped petals that both incurve and hood. The perianth is a fairly light yellow that fades to cream and the cup a few shades darker. However it is fertile, and might be used to produce something better. I have lost 'Picarillo' three times, and finally decided not to replace it. It is a lemon-yellow self and has prominently incurved petals. 'Tweeny' (Gray) is an elusive thing. It rarely blooms, and to further complicate matters, when it does, it is generally 'Yellow Xit'. Apparently a large number of bulbs of 'Yellow Xit' were marketed some years ago under the name of 'Tweeny'. I have had bulbs of this for twenty-odd years, but I think mine, too, is not 'Tweeny', at it does not match Gray's description. Unless it is growing somewhere in England, I think that the real 'Tweeny' is probably lost. Recently registered 'Northam' 2W-W (formerly MJB212B) is another rather large flower on a short stem. It is really a failed trumpet, and does not have good form or clear white colour. The two best of the group of larger flowers are 'Picoblanco', 2W-W (Gray) and 'Sewanee', 2W-Y (Watrous). 'Picoblanco' is a reliable early-midseason flower, whiter than any but 'Xit', with fair form. It needs to be cut young for showing. It is not easy to establish, but grows very well when acclimatized. I have two forms of this cultivar, the better one being the one (of course!) which increases very slowly. Roberta Watrous' 'Sewanee' is a large-cupped edition of 'Segovia', and a very good flower, about the size of 'Segovia'. It has a brilliant white perianth, clear yellow cup and good show form, which makes it indispensable to the exhibitor. A good grower and increaser, it has reputedly set seed occasionally.

Then, there is a group of four really tiny flowers, none of which is widely known. 'Rosaline Murphy', 2Y-Y, is so early that it is rarely seen in shows, and can be easily missed in the garden too, as it is so short it often blooms under my mulch. It is a true division 2 flower with good form, a very pale self yellow about 22mm (1in) in diameter, and is very lovely, but quite fragile. Carl Teschner, a botanist in New Zealand, registered two 2Y-Ys some years ago. His 'Yimkin' is now being seen at shows in the USA. 'Niade', another tiny self yellow will follow it soon, as it is seen more. Both have very narrow perianth segments, so are starry looking. So far, they are proving to be good growers. They are just as small as 'Rosaline Murphy' and are about the same height 7.5cm (3in). Last is John Blanchard's recent registration of a cross made in 1959, 'Nimlet', 2Y-Y. I first saw this in England last year and hope to grow it some day, but I understand it is a very slow increaser.

Division 3.
The division 3 flowers are a group of six larger, rather tall flowers. 'Segovia', 'Xit' and 'Yellow Xit' are almost too well-known to describe, except that there is some confusion about the differences between 'Segovia' and 'Yellow Xit'. It is easy to tell them apart when they are seen together - 'Segovia' has a much whiter perianth, and, on opening, a slightly brighter yellow cup,

but when mature the cup colours are nearly identical. The perianth of 'Yellow Xit' has a definite greenish cast to it. Both perianths tend to reflex slightly as the flowers age, especially 'Yellow Xit'. 'Xit', 3W-W, has a brilliant white perianth with a flat, lightly fluted cup that is sometimes lobed. (the margin of the cup exhibits the same variability as its parent, *N. rupicola* subsp. *watieri*). These three flowers have probably won more Best Miniature in show awards in the USA than any others and are indispensable to the miniature grower. There is another form of 'Xit', the last clone (let us hope!) to be found and separated from the grex that produced the three above. This is a slightly shorter plant, with a distinctly greenish-white perianth and cup. The cup is a shallow bowl shape, is not fluted, and the rim is entire. It has now been registered as 'Exit', 3W-W, an appropriate name for the last of the "Xit Bunch". 'Paula Cottell', 3W-GWW, blooms later than the rest, so is most useful for late shows. It is close to the others in height and flower size, and has a lovely green eye. In cold seasons the cup can open very yellow, but it fades quickly. A recent addition to the small cups is Mary Lou Gripshover's 'Three of Diamonds', 3W-GWO with a "diamond-dusted" perianth and lovely cup colour. For me, it grows a bit too large to be a true miniature.

Division 4.
Now, I am in trouble, double trouble, for flowers from division 4 rarely bloom for me. My climate has too many sudden temperature swings, - up in the 80s during the day, then into the low 20s at night, sometimes even in early spring. Doubles just can't do their thing under such circumstances, and they blast. They need a warmer climate, or more protection (than I can give them) in colder ones. I have grown 'Kehelland', 'Pencrebar' and 'Wren' for over 20 years, and doubt if I have had a total of ten flowers from the lot in all that time, and often, these were deformed. All are deep yellow, and rather large for the stem height. 'Wren' is by far the best, having a much more orderly arrangement of the perianth and coronal segments.

'Flore Pleno' and 'Eystettensis' are slightly more reliable bloomers for me. 'Eystettensis 'is rarely in top form, but when it is, it is lovely, and so distinctive, with its graduated pale yellow petaloids exactly aligned one on top of another. 'Jonquil Flore Pleno' can produce good flowers occasionally, on a rather tall stem. 'Rip van Winkle' (now the official name for all the "plenuses") is very aptly named - he looks as if he had been sleeping rather more than 20 years, and has gone far beyond any hope of ever looking neat! I have never seen a style, or anthers, on any of these in my garden.

Not to put too fine a point on it, dear hybridizers, nowhere in the daffodil world is there an area in greater need of your attentions. Only two of this group come from recent crosses! Broadening the range of colour and improved form and vigour are especially needed, also lengthening the season. As mentioned elsewhere, breeders in several areas are working on improving miniatures, but their work seems to be concentrated in a few divisions -divisions 1, 5 and 6, mainly. No one appears to be concentrating on divisions 2 and 3, where the lack of good cultivars is most evident.

So, in conclusion, I issue herewith a challenge to all hybridizers everywhere, to rectify this sorry *lacuna*. There **are** fertile miniatures capable of producing good flowers, particularly in the much-needed divisions 2 and 3. Some excellent potential parents are: *N. rupicola* subsp. *watieri,* 13W-W, *N. cuatrecasasii* 13Y-Y (especially the better forms), the good white miniature trumpets, possibly 'Picoblanco' (fertility unknown) and intermediate division 2 cultivars like 'Bantam' and 'Scarlet Tanager', 'Fairy Circle', 'Dinkie' and other small division 3 cultivars and the smallest poets. Last, but hardly least, is 'Pequenita', a fertile (both ways) and very beautiful 7Y-Y that has all the characteristics of a fine division 2 flower of the shorter cupped type, with the additional advantage of one white and one yellow parent. Most of these cultivars are not that difficult to find, so, please, let's begin working for more and better miniatures in these divisions!

More AGM Daffodils and Tulips

Wisley Daffodil Trials 1999

David Matthews

This year at Wisley the Committee had only two small beds to view, there being 33 cultivars in total. Overall health of the plants had improved this Spring, although unfortunately basal rot had accounted for two complete stocks in one bed. The main Trials for the year 2000 had been hot water treated so these 67 cultivars were not assessed this year, but a number of bulbs suffering from virus and basal rot had to be removed. Members of the Trials Committee, together with the staff at Wisley have discussed the problems however, and are confident they can be overcome.

At the recent Trials Sub-Committee Meeting the chairman Brian Duncan announced the resignations of Noel Burr and Jim Pearce. Noel Burr had served since 1983, and Jim Pearce had served for 16 years, during which time he had been chairman from 1985-1994 and vice-chairman to date. Alan Hardy who sadly had died in February had also been a long serving member of the Sub-Committee. These three gentlemen will all be greatly missed for their vast knowledge and experience in daffodil cultivation, and their constant interest in the Trials at Wisley.

Award of Garden Merit

At the 9 June 1999 meeting of the Daffodil and Tulip Trials Sub-Committee recommendations were made that five cultivars be awarded the Award of Garden Merit as a flowering plant for garden decoration. Brief comments by the Committee on each cultivar are shown in italics. Thanks are due to the Wisley staff who furnished the flowering periods and the number of flowers recorded.

Narcissus **'Dispatch Box'** 1Y-Y sent for trial by Mr B S Duncan, Knowehead, 15 Ballynahatty Road, Omagh, Co Tyrone BT78 1PN. *"An outstanding garden cultivar; very free flowering with flower held well above the robust foliage. Tremendous impact. Flowered from 22.3.99 to 16.4.99 with 85 stems from 23 bulbs".*

Narcissus **'Serena Lodge'** 4W-Y sent for trial by Mr B S Duncan. *"An ideal garden variety with good impact; stands up to the weather very well for a double due to its short neck and stout stem which account for the flower's good poise. Flowers over a long period'. Flowered from 4.4.99 to 28.4.99 with 135 stems from 25 bulbs".*

Narcissus **'Chesterton'** 9W-GYR sent for trial by Mr B S Duncan. *"The flower colour, form and foliage make this cultivar ideal for garden cultivation. A slightly smaller bloom than 'Cantabile', it stands up well to the weather with only a slight burning to the cup being noted. Flowered from 14.4.99 to 30.4.99 with 90 flowering stems from 23 bulbs".*

Narcissus **'Notre Dame'** 2W-GYP sent for trial by Mr B S Duncan. *"A late flowering variety with a long flowering period, a lovely blend of colours which did not burn in the sun, and an excellent flower count recorded'. Flowered from 6.8.99 to 4.5.99 with 145 stems from 25 bulbs".*

Narcissus **'Highfield Beauty'** 8Y-YYO sent for trial by Mr B S Duncan. *"A tall, strong growing variety. Very weather resistant with an extremely strong constitution. The two to four flowers per stem are held with good poise and did not burn in the sun. Flowered from 24.3.99 to 12.4.99 with 85 flowering stems from 24 bulbs".*

AGM Tulips

James L Akers

Two previous visits to Holland have been made by members of the Daffodil and Tulip Committee of the Royal Horticultural Society to assess tulips for the RHS Award of Garden Merit. The visit in April 1997 enabled selection to be made mainly from the early flowering Fosteriana and Greigii hybrid groups and that in May 1995 was mainly concerned with late flowering cultivars. On this occasion the large range of mid-season cultivars was the target and as it turned out the season was perfect.

The assessment team (see Fig. 13) on 27 to 30 April 1999 consisted of B Duncan, D J Pearce, J W Blanchard, W Lemmers, R Blom, D Matthews and the writer and we were ably directed by the secretary of the Daffodil and Tulip Committee, Sally Kington. The chairman of the Royal General Bulb Growers Association, Sjaak Langeslag and the international tulip registrar, Johan van Scheepen were entertained to dinner. The procedure for assessing and scoring the cultivars is described in the *Yearbook 1997-8* page 81.

As in previous years the tulips were seen in the Keukenhof and Hortus Bulborum gardens, the Hobaho trial grounds and the private collection of Cees Breed who was co-opted to the selection committee. We were able also to see daffodils and species tulips in the fields of Messrs Meeuwissen. Those of us who try with varying degrees of success to grow a pot of six species tulips for show could only marvel at the sight of rows of these tulips 150m (167yds) long and 120cm (4ft) wide all the same height and in perfect condition (see Fig. 22). For several in the party it was the most enduring sight of the three days. As a result of the visit, five daffodils were put forward for trial at Wisley and comments submitted on six already in trial. The 32 tulips which were recommended for AGM are shown here by group, indicating the number of AGM tulips now in the group.

Single Early Group (4)
'Apricot Beauty' *Salmon rose, tinged red*
Double Early Group (4)
'Fringed Beauty' *Vermilion, fringed yellow*
Triumph Group (36)
'Barcelona' *Fuschia purple* (see Fig. 21)
'Blue Bell' *Orchid purple*
'Etude' *Blood red, edged yellow*
'Friso' *Blood red with cardinal red flame*
'Holberg' *Doge purple*
'Lily Schreyer' *Flamed canary yellow on darker shade*
'Monte Rosa' *Flamed carmine rose and rosy white*
'Musical' *Cardinal red*
'Orleans' *Mimosa yellow flame on white*
'Sevilla' *China rose*
'Strong Gold' *Primrose yellow with orange flame*
'Ted Turner' *Canary yellow*
'Valentine' *Tyrian purple with white edge*
Darwinhybrid Group (21)
'Ollioules' *Jasper red with green stripes*
'Tender Beauty' *Rosy red and white*
'Vivex' *Carmine rose, edged orange yellow*
Single Late Group (19)
'World Expression' *Primrose yellow*
Lily Flowered Group (9)
'Synaeda King' *Current red with broad yellow edge*
Fringed Group (9)
'Crystal Beauty' *Claret rose with orange fringe*
'Fringed Elegance' *Primrose yellow with pink dots*
Viridiflora Group (4)
Esperanto *China rose, midrib flamed green*
Double Late Group (6)
'Angélique' *Pale pink with darker shades*
'Carnaval de Nice' *White, red striped*
'Gerbrand Kieft' *Purple red, edged white*
'Maywonder' *Rose*
Fosteriana Group (8)
'Flaming Youth' *Vermilion red*
Greigii Group (32)
'Grand Prestige' *Bright vermilion*
'Smyrna' *Deep cardinal red, edged yellow*
Miscellaneous (17)
Tulipa clusiana 'Cynthia' *Spinel red, edged green*
Tulipa whittallii *Bright orange, green and buff*

No further awards were made in the **Kaufmanniana** (7) and **Parrot** (3) groups.

Cyclamineus Hybrids in the Garden

Christine Skelmersdale

The smaller daffodils have undergone a quiet revolution during the past years and none more so than the graceful cyclamineus cultivars. The older hybrids, such as 'Peeping Tom' and 'Jenny' have always been popular, if rather expensive when compared to other daffodils but improved propagation methods, dramatic new varieties and rising public awareness have propelled division 6 into the limelight.

N. cyclamineus, from which all have take their characteristic slender, nodding trumpet and more or less reflexed perianth, has yet another character that makes its progeny so excellent for British gardens - a liking for cool, damp soils. This is clearly demonstrated in the moist woodland margins at Wisley, where *N. cyclamineus* has seeded in thousands. Its other preference, for an acid soil, lessens as the influence of *N. cyclamineus* in its ancestry diminishes. As a rule of thumb I find that the smaller the hybrid the more likely it is to prefer an acid soil. Division 6 hybrids can therefore, for purely horticultural purposes, be separated into two categories - the small, near species cultivars and the larger more robust ones.

Delicate hybrids, such as 'Mite', 'Mitzy' and 'Cedric Nice', all require a cool, acid soil that is not too dry and are ideal for growing among shrubs, although some of the smallest, such as 'Minicycla' and 'Snipe', may require some frost protection. All quickly increase to form large clumps that benefit from regular division. This can be done with no detriment to subsequent flowering, when the leaves first appear or after flowering as the leaves fade in late spring. I find that trying to locate dormant clumps can be fraught with danger and almost inevitably leads to some damaged bulbs.

The newer dwarf hybrids, such as 'Hummingbird' and 'Swift Arrow', are probably also better grown out of doors as we find them rather intolerant of pan culture, but as yet our stocks are too small to risk. In gardens with a sizeable species population some natural hybrids will arise, although few have any great merit all display a delicate charm and are a welcome serendipity. However chance hybrids should not be named 'Minicycla', as this name refers to a specific cultivar.

Although now re-registered as division 12, the well-known trio of 'Tête-à-Tête', 'Jumblie' and 'Quince', having a shared tazetta and cyclamineus ancestry, also prefer a neutral to acid soil, tending to fade away on dry, limey soils. Each of these varieties produces multiple flower stems, the majority of which are multi-headed. At 15cm (6in) to 20cm (8in) they are very wind resistant and, coupled with their early flowering, this makes them one of the best subjects for containers, both indoors and out.

Similar soil pH restrictions do not apply to the larger hybrids. Like their smaller counterparts they too are early flowering and grow well in cool, woodland conditions where there is plenty of light early in the season. It is here that I grow some of the more recent hybrids, such as, 'Foundling', 'Cha-Cha' and 'Mary Lou'. The latter definitely prefers this situation. A clump in the open gradually faded away and the delicate pink colour seems more at home in the muted atmosphere of the shrubbery. Other good cultivars are the bicoloured 'Noss Mayo' (see Fig. 8), 'Tracey', 'Trena' (see Fig. 11) and 'Toby the First' and the yellow self 'The Alliance'.

Unlike *N. cyclamineus* itself, which is rarely truly happy in grass, most of the larger cultivars revel in it and provide some of the best subjects for naturalising. They combine vigour with the other desirable qualities of early flowering and a graceful appearance. The latter being especially important in a more natural setting where some of the larger hybrids may look out of place. When planting in grass an allowance should be made for the rapid rate of increase of these varieties. The ideal spacing is around 23cm (9in) to 30cm (12in) between bulbs. The planting will appear thin for the first few years but the gaps will soon close and it reduces the need for frequent lifting and dividing of congested and consequently blind plants. 'February Gold', 'Jack Snipe' (see Fig. 7), 'Jenny', 'Peeping Tom' and 'Little Witch' are all proven varieties for this situation, even on dry soils.

With a liking for such varied conditions, it is probably not surprising that division 6 dominates the daffodils in my garden.

CARLO ALBERTO NAEF
1902-1997

Carlo Alberto Naef – "The Guv'nor"

Jan Dalton

Carlo Naef was not just a professional in the flower marketing trade but more an institution in his own right. He was, or perhaps more correctly, he became, J & E Page & Co Ltd that most famous of flower firms concerned with London's Covent Garden Market and the cut flower industry.

As we know from his obituary in last year's *Yearbook*, Carlo was born in Livorno on the coast of Tuscany, Italy on 29 May 1902. His Swiss father Karl, himself a successful businessman exporting Carrara marble, medicinal plants, olive oil and the wines of Tuscany to America was determined that his eldest son Carlo would become fluent in several European languages and receive tuition in the piano, dancing, sport and the art of shooting.

Following his education in Switzerland and playing team football throughout Europe, Carlo eventually began work in a Swiss import/export business belonging to Otto Jaeger a close friend of his father. Carlo's linguistic skills stood him in good stead and he soon adapted their use to his firm's communications system by devising a unique telegraphic code in four languages that was to prove a substantial saving in time and money. Jaegers had branches in New York, London, Paris and Singapore and in the early 1920s Carlo was sent to work at the London office. It was during this time that Carlo met his first wife Pet (Madge), though it was only through his own determination, an enforced six months spell in the Swiss Army and an unprecedented snub of his fathers and his employer's wishes that the two were to become man and wife. It also led Carlo to adopt England as his new home and to take up a job with his father-in-law Edward Page's business, J & E Page of Covent Garden.

Carlo's new job at J & E Page was as a junior clerk but this was not to last long for someone as ambitious and worldly wise as Carlo. He wanted to become a flower salesman "on the floor" at Covent Garden and it was once again his determination that won the day, though he had to begin as a porter and learn the skills from scratch. In 1928 Edward Page underwent major surgery and did not return to the helm until the following year, and then only part-time. The firm became a limited company with Carlo as its first Company Secretary. Difficult times followed during the slump of the late 1920s and Carlo worked long hours, often from 3am to early evening with growers' returns to be dealt with once back at home. In 1936 his hard work was rewarded with a directorship of the firm. During the war, Edward Page died and Carlo purchased sufficient shares to become the largest stockholder and Managing Director of J & E Page. From office boy to top man in just 18 years.

For most people this would have been sufficient achievement for one lifetime and yet the amazing part of this story was still to unfold, as far as the RHS and the daffodil world were concerned. Carlo first joined the RHS Narcissus and Tulip Committee in 1958 at the age of 56. In keeping with his many professional attributes, Carlo remained loyal to this committee for a staggering 35 years, until his "retirement" in 1992 at the age of 90! During this time Carlo brought to the committee the benefits of his long experience in the cut flower trade and his wide knowledge of daffodils and tulips as a commercial crop led to the publishing of many detailed, informative articles on the subject in the *Yearbooks* and other horticultural publications.

Ever alert to market movements and his wish to present the best quality flowers to the

15

general public, Carl helped to pioneer the sale of cut daffodils in "goose-neck" and later "pencil" stages of growth over 35 years ago. A revolution that streamlined the flower picking and packing process and meant that the customer could expect maximum vase life from their purchases. Carlo was very much opposed to the cold storage of open blooms by the growers and one of his many favourite sayings went something like "the grower has no business to see his crop when it is most beautiful, he must pick and market it long before he can truly enjoy it himself". His remarkable ability to adopt, adapt or even invent something which would overcome a problem was no better illustrated than by his design of a special clip that reinforced and held together the vulnerable point of the wooden flower boxes used in the trade. Millions of these were made, though as Carlo said it was not one of his best business moves as he never patented the clip.

Carlo continued to head the firm even into his 80s and was always in touch with the office by phone to say "Hello, the Guv'nor here - how did sales go today?". Indeed, a weekly visit to the office kept him abreast of the company's operation, which by the 1990s had become the second largest cut flower wholesale company in the United Kingdom. The Page Group of which Carlo was Chairman now had branches in the markets at Gateshead, Preston and Merthyr Tydfil and diversified into flower importing and distribution, transporting and exotic produce.

For his long and dedicated service to the flower industry and in particular to the daffodil, Carlo received numerous accolades and honours, among them:

"Man of the Year"

The Peter Barr Memorial Cup

Officer of the Most Excellent Order of the British Empire (OBE) 1981

His appointments and achievements are too numerous to mention, though he placed more importance on his relationships with people, in particular his beloved family. Throughout his life Carlo had a favourite prayer that was the maxim by which he lived:

God grant me the serenity to accept things that I cannot change,
Courage to change the things that I can,
And the wisdom to know the difference.

Carlo loved his family, his children and his grandchildren and taught them all this prayer. Sadly, both he and his family and friends would have cause to call on this prayer for strength to over come life's cruel side. Carlo's first wife Pet (Madge) passed away when still quite young and some years later in 1958 their daughter June and son-in-law were both killed in a car accident. Tragically, history was to repeat itself in 1992 when June's son Patrick Hackett, Carlo's grandson, was also killed in a car accident. This was a devastating blow to Carlo who had just celebrated his 90th birthday at a special event organised by Patrick at the Savoy Hotel, London. Carlo had also just seen Patrick take over the reins at J & E Page. Then, in recent years Carlo's second wife Helen (Ellen as he wrote it) also died. The story ended in October 1997, when after a short illness, Carlo died at the age of 95. A great man, always willing to help anyone in need, always an optimist and always "the Guv'nor".

Carlo was many things to many people and my own abiding memory of him was when I first joined the RHS Narcissus and Tulip Committee 11 years ago. I remember gazing in awe and respect at the assembled company of people, David Lloyd, Sir Arundel Neave, Bob Southon, Walter Stagg, Fred Shepherd, Beatrice Coleman, Millar Gault, all sadly no longer with us. It was Carlo who leaned across and whispered words of reassurance and encouragement. From that day I always had a great admiration for Carlo and will always remember his support of the "new" face on the committee. My endearing recollection of Carlo has to be at Chelsea Flower Show where he always turned up immaculately dressed complete with Panama hat, buttonhole and shooting stick and his wonderful gentlemanly manner of doffing his hat to every lady that spoke to him. Those days are fast disappearing, though we will always remember people like Carlo, they have that effect on you.

Growing Snowdrops

John Grimshaw

I have been asked to write a short piece on how I grow snowdrops. .. The simple answer is that I plant them in the ground and leave them there, but that would make a rather shorter article than editor was expecting, so I shall have to spin it out a bit.

Snowdrops have become incredibly popular in recent years - deservedly so, as there are few other plants that so effectively cheer up the dull days of winter. Despite the apparent similarity of their flowers and habit, enthusiasts - galanthophiles - have named some 700 cultivars, and the number grows every season. This is not the place to go into details - a book is in progress - so I shall assume a basic knowledge of what a snowdrop is and confine my remarks to some of *my* ideas about growing them - others will doubtless disagree.

Snowdrops are very adaptable plants, and seldom need special attention - they can indeed be poked in and left to their own devices with considerable success. Visitors to the garden of the late Primrose Warburg in Oxford who admired the drifts of choice snowdrops in her wood in February, would have been astonished to see the same places in July, when the ground was occupied by a waving thicket of nettles and horsetails. A coarse mowing in late summer was sufficient to ensure that the snowdrops and other bulbs could emerge free of an overburden of stems and hay. Such a regime fits the lifecycle of a *Galanthus* perfectly. Light for photosynthesis is essential during the growing season - January to April or early May, by when the foliage is senescent and dies away, leaving a dormant bulb to rest through the summer. What happens over its head is of no consequence to it at that time, and the toughened shoot tips can easily penetrate a tangle of roots as they emerge, so there is no real competition between the snowdrops and other plants.

Here (southern England) I grow my snowdrops in the slightly tamer situations of mixed borders of shrubs and herbaceous plants that form a fairly dense tangle throughout the summer, but are clear during the winter and early spring. I am particularly fond of promoting the cultivation of snowdrops under rose bushes, whether shrub roses or modem hybrids. Beds of the latter, cut down to a series of spiky stumps, are to me an appalling eyesore for most of the year, and cry out for something of interest during the winter months. A carpet of small bulbs under them works wonders, and causes no harm whatsoever to the roses. The bushes are free of leaves all winter, but provide shade and abstract moisture during the summer, providing cool dry resting conditions for the bulbs, while a mulch of garden compost applied in summer benefits both shrubs and bulbs. Some enthusiasts grow snowdrops in splendid isolation, but I prefer to intersperse them with other early-flowering plants such as *Crocus tommasinianus, Cyclamen coum* and *Eranthis hyemalis* to make a bright mass of flowers. If you are growing a collection of named cultivars it is critical, however, to ensure that clumps of snowdrops are well spaced from each other, and permanently labelled. Otherwise clumps merge, identities are lost and muddles are made that are not easily sorted out. Misnamed snowdrops, even when obtained from an expert, are not at all infrequent!

There is some dispute amongst galanthophiles about the desirability of soil improvements, with some evidence to suggest that addition of mulches of mushroom compost or bark causes disease and losses, while inorganic fertilisers also seem to encourage viral disease. *Galanthus* pathology, although a real concern, has most often been swept under the carpet and we are very ignorant of both the diseases and their causes or cures. Standard advice has been to destroy the affected bulb, but many have been reluctant to destroy a bulb for which several pounds have been paid and it has been planted in a "distant" corner of the garden. Miracle cures, when the striping has disappeared, are often reported, but viruses don't just go away like that They remain, and spread. We do not even know the vectors of the several viruses that affect snowdrops, and nobody has conclusively proved that virus can spread from *Narcissus* to *Galanthus,* although I and several others think they can. Here, where I grow a very wide range of plants above the snowdrops on a basically fertile neutral loam, I apply mulches of garden compost when I can, a general scattering of bone meal in autumn, and a dose of Growmore in about April, when the snowdrops are dying back and are hopefully not going to be affected by it. There are traces of virus in some clones, but the majority seem to thrive.

Some snowdrops do have special requirements and these I try to provide. The majority of species and hybrids grow happily throughout the garden, wherever there was a space when I acquired the plant, but even with commoner species I have certain ideas of where they want to be. For example, I believe that G. *nivalis,* G. *plicatus* and their cultivars and hybrids, prefer a site that is not too hot in summer, and they tend to get planted under the shrub roses and in cooler borders. G. *elwesii,* the other most commonly grown species, seems to prefer a warm summer rest, so it goes in the west facing border, or on the rock garden, where a warm dry summer rest is more likely. Similarly, G. *reginae-olgae,* the Greek autumn-flowering species, appreciates a warm summer rest and is a rock garden species. It is no coincidence that warm places in summer are also warmer and sunnier in winter, and these early flowering plants also benefit from maximum exposure to the sun in January. Conversely, some of the rarer species from the Caucasus, such as G. *alpinus,* G. *platyphyllus* and G. *krasnowii* like a cool, humus rich site that does not dry out in summer, so they are planted in my peat bed. The yellow-marked G. *nivalis* 'Sandersii', which is often regarded as a rather feeble grower, also seems to enjoy such a site, but it may also be responding to the increased attention it receives in a choice spot.

The first step in growing snowdrops is to acquire them. Standard advice is to plant them "in the green", while actively growing in spring, a practice that became widespread following its adoption by the Giant Snowdrop Company in the 1950s. Unlike the dismal success rate from the moribund bulbs imported by the million from Turkey and sold in autumn by bulb merchants (a trade fortunately now regulated by CITES), snowdrops in the green could be seen to survive and grow. There is no doubt that it is a very successful method, and the vast majority of my plants have been acquired in this state. For one thing, the plants are visible and easily extracted, while the recipient can choose a site for them with little trouble. Secondly, a purchaser of often expensive bulbs can be sure that the correct cultivar is received, and a visible "plant" is much more satisfying than a little dry bulb. A growing plant lifted from the ground, bundled in plastic and sent by post is, however, a stressed plant, and needs care that is frequently not given. I have often seen, even in the gardens of other galanthophiles, newly planted snowdrops flagging or wilted from lack of water. A lot of roots get broken or even dried-up on transplantation, so it is essential that they are watered copiously on planting and when necessary thereafter until they become dormant

I now advocate and practice the transplantation of snowdrops while dormant in summer, like any other winter-growing bulbs, and find that it is very successful. People seem to expect this to be immediately fatal - it is not. The enemy of snowdrop bulbs is desiccation, not the act of lifting. It is not surprising that

Turkish imports were such a poor buy; they had usually been lifted in full growth dried off in the sun and stored in warehouses before despatch to the customer. Most were dead on arrival. If desiccation is avoided, snowdrops can be lifted, stored and dispatched at any time during their dormant period. Storage in peat or sand works well, and bulbs replanted as late as October will flower normally next year. Early replanting is best, however, and the ground should be firmed and watered to ensure that the bulbs are not sitting in a pocket of loose dry soil in which they can also become desiccated. Root growth will commence as soon as the soil cools in late summer, so it is best to lift as soon as possible after the bulbs become dormant.

Propagation has traditionally been by division of the bulbs, a slow process that has meant that many choice cultivars have remained scarce and sought after, commanding high prices when they appear for sale. In recent years twin-scaling has been widely applied to snowdrops with great success, and desirable clones have become more freely available but no cheaper! Galanthophilia can become an expensive obsession, but in moderation, like most pleasures, is a wonderful ailment to suffer from. Plant some snowdrops now!

The home of Narcissus Ajax Cyclamineus.

Drawing taken from the front of Barr's Daffodils *1887*

N. CYCLAMINEUS AND ITS HYBRIDS – A SYMPOSIUM

This year's symposium takes a wide ranging look at *N. cyclamineus* and its hybrids in division 6. Including synonyms and species there were 27,050 entries in the International Daffodil Register in June 1999, of which only 378 (1.4%) relate to division 6. However, such small numbers understate the popularity of cyclamineus hybrids amongst gardeners, exhibitors and hybridizers. Here can be found flowers whose graceful but informal and distinctive form contrasts sharply with the starched geometric perfection of modern standard sized daffodils in division 1 - 3. Similarly, against a background of new cultivars which often flower in late mid-season, cyclamineus hybrids still mostly live up to the poets assertion that daffodils are the "harbinger of Spring". Also, as Christine Skelmersdale points out on page 13 cyclamineus hybrids remain in flower for a long time, thrive in our damp climate and are well suited to small gardens.

Many years ago, the late John Lea showed a superb bloom of 'Charity May' 6Y-Y which was an unsuccessful but strong contender for the Best Bloom award at a major London show. However, despite receiving such awards abroad, a cyclamineus hybrid has yet to be judged Best Bloom at a major national show in the United Kingdom. This said, cyclamineus hybrids have done well at such shows when it comes to selecting the Best Bloom from divisions 5-9. In the last decade, 'Tiger Moth' 6W-P, 'Elfin Gold' 6Y-Y, 'Lilac Charm' 6W-GPP, 'Suzie Dee' 6Y-Y, 'The Alliance' 6Y-Y and 'Rapture' 6Y-Y have all received such awards. An obvious comment is that many division 6 cultivars are past their best by the time mid and late season shows take place. This problem is further compounded by the absence of separate classes for miniatures from division 6 at shows in the United Kingdom. Forced into single bloom classes with a wide coverage miniature cyclamineus hybrids tend to lose out to cultivars from divisions 5 and 7.

The emergence of the RHS Early Daffodil Competition in London has been a welcome development for exhibitors of cyclamineus hybrids. Amongst standard sized cultivars, the more favourable show date has been reflected in a Best Bloom in show award to 'Trena' 6W-Y (see Fig. 11) this year and a Reserve Best Bloom in show award to 'Carclew' 6Y-Y in 1996. Both flowers were exhibited by Ron Scamp who grows his daffodils in West Cornwall, an area with one of the earliest flowering seasons in the United Kingdom. A similar story can be told in respect of miniatures, where John Blanchard's diminutive seedling 83/32A (*N. asturiensis* x *N. cyclamineus*) received the Best Bloom in show award in 1996.

This year, our cultivar surveys by Malcolm Bradbury, Janine Doulton, Delia Bankhead, Richard Perrignon and David Adams are followed by a further contribution from Delia about miniature cyclamineus hybrids and from John Blanchard about judging. The cultivar surveys are preceded by contributions from Malcolm Bradbury on "Breeding Activity and Problems" and "*N. cyclamineus* in the Wild".

BREEDING ACTIVITY AND PROBLEMS

MALCOLM BRADBURY

A Lot of Breeding Activity
A comparison of hybridizing activity in divisions 5 and 6 reveals an interesting change in

their relative popularity. Last year, we noted 481 cultivars in division 5 compared to the 378 currently registered in division 6. Conversely, we also noted that between the start of 1987 and the end of June 1997, 23 cultivars, raised by twelve hybridizers had been registered in division 5. In the case of division 6, no less than 98 cultivars were registered by at least 33 hybridizers between the start of 1990 and the middle of June this year. The comparisons are not exact, but two conclusions stand out; division 5 cultivars are less popular than they used to be and division 6 cultivars are increasing rapidly in popularity. This record of recent hybridizing activity also confirms the impression given in our surveys of an active interest in breeding miniature as well as standard division 6 cultivars.

Given the fertility problems associated with triploids, the fact that at least 61 of the new registrations record *N. cyclamineus* as being one of the parents is no surprise. The remainder involve the full range of possibilities noted by Peter Brandham (see page 29) and taken at face value add to the impression that a significant number of fertile cultivars are available in division 6.

Form and poise

For good practical reasons, registration is based on the appearance and not the parentage of a cultivar. This said, the characteristics of *N. cyclamineus* are expected to be "clearly evident" in cultivars registered in division 6, however, not all the characteristics in question need be represented. For example, *N. cyclamineus* has a rounded stem, but many of its hybrids do not. Space does not permit a full discussion of the many issues surrounding the exclusion or inclusion of cultivars from this division. Having moved cultivars where perianths do not reflex or which are multi-headed, debate has particularly focused on how perianths reflex, petal width, corona length and width and the overall height and size of the stem and flower.

Even where there is no doubt about the inclusion of *N. cyclamineus* as a parent almost all of the above issues can arise in the resulting hybrids. First, any hybrid will inherit some characteristics from each parent. Thus for example seedlings of 'Bryanston' × *N. cyclamineus* which I flowered this year varied considerably in stem length, flower size, perianth reflex and corona shape. Second, if we cross *N. cyclamineus* with a division 1 cultivar we should expect different results than if for example the cross involves cultivars from divisions 3 and 9. Obvious illustrations of this point are 'Peeping Tom' and 'Perky', where one parent was from division 1 and 'Crofty' (see Fig. 5) and 'Beryl' where the other parents were from divisions 3 and 9 respectively. These variations in form and poise simply reflect similar differences between cultivars in the divisions in question.

A more difficult issue arises where there are doubts about whether *N. cyclamineus* features at all in the parentage of a hybrid. Many such hybrids are both visually attractive and fertile and hence of interest to hybridizers. The obvious question here, is that either the cyclamineus characteristics are likely to be unconvincing or can be partly obtained via another route ie parents derived from the *N. poeticus* group. In this instance I remain unconvinced; either because perianths in the *N. poeticus* group do not reflex in quite the same way as *N. cyclamineus*, or because it is not clear where other relevant characteristics might come from.

The unresolved problem, is that hybridizers have created a group of attractive and fertile cultivars which currently reside with varying degrees of unease in division 6. Simple solutions do not exist and in many instances opinions are legitimately divided. Movement into divisions 1, 2 and 3 implies commercial death in show terms until schedules include classes for intermediate sized cultivars with reflexing petals. Similarly recreating the pre 1977 subdivisions of cyclamineus hybrids based on the relationship between perianth and corona length would help but is not a perfect solution.

Practical problems.

Standard advice to daffodil hybridizers is that

21

only a few seedlings (say less than one in a hundred) will be good enough to name. In the case of first generation cyclamineus hybrids the odds are probably much worse given the many constraints expressed by crossing such dissimilar parents. In the absence of fertility problems breeding cyclamineus hybrids would ultimately be no more difficult than breeding daffodils in divisions 1-3. Over many generations it would be possible to select parents which both included N. cyclamineus in their parentage and to fix and refine desired characteristics. Similarly unwanted characteristics could be bred out.

The low fertility of first generation cyclamineus hybrids creates two problems. First, where the cross involves another daffodil from division 1-3 the resulting cultivars show less cyclamineus characteristics, increase in size and lose the grace associated with the species. 'Joybell' ('Jenny' open-pollinated) is a typical example of this outcome. Second, since typically only a few seeds are obtained, hybridizers often have insufficient seedlings available from which to make proper choices.

In the case of miniatures, crossing diploids is an obvious possible way forward. With standard sized division 6 cultivars, two choices are available. Follow Peter Brandham's advice and hope for a break-through. Alternatively be convinced that the break-through has already happened and that *N. cyclamineus* does indeed feature significantly in the parentage of some of the fertile cultivars that Peter identifies.

N. *CYCLAMINEUS* IN THE WILD

Malcolm Bradbury

With its natural habitat along tributaries of the river Douro in Northern Portugal and in North West Spain under pressure from flooding, cultivation and urban development, *N. cyclamineus* is now very rare in the wild. It has not been seen by those modern authorities who write about wild daffodils, though it is said to survive in the wild on a few large private estates. Consequently we have to rely on observations made by those who rediscovered *N. cyclamineus* in the 1880s and on experience of the species in cultivation.

Though not a botanist, Alfred W Tait the British Consul at Oporto in Portugal, corresponded with friends in England about the wild daffodils he found nearby. Eventually this led in 1886 to the publication of a brief resume of his observations made during the years 1885 and 1886[1]. He recalled that *N. cyclamineus* grew near Oporto on the banks of a stream, flowering between 28 February and 10 March at an altitude of about 90m (300ft). Tait went on to say that "A flower of this rare plant was first shown to me by my friend Mr Edwin Johnston and on visiting the locality I found a fairly abundant supply of plants though it appears to be confined to this locality."

Subsequently in 1889, Tait gave a more comprehensive description of *N. cyclamineus* which he had seen during trips made earlier that year[2]. In the absence of more recent published evidence Tait's note is reprinted in full below.

"*Cyclamineus.* - These began flowering about the first week in February, and are still in flower (April 12). We have met with three new localities for this beautiful species, all near Oporto.

The original habitat described and figured by Mr Barr two years ago (*see picture on page 19 - Editor*), was a striking sight this year; thousands of the golden blooms carpeted the river bank, mixed with primroses and bushes of the tall white heath (*Erica arborea*).

Up till the present I have met with the following varieties of cyclamineus:-
1. A perfectly double-flowered form. The flower resembled that of the common Dutch double Jonquilla, but was larger, and of a greenish yellow, like Telamonius plenus. I found only a single specimen of this and it has since flowered in the Coimbra Botanic Gardens, still with the double flower.
2. One or two specimens with the cup double.

3. Several specimens with two-flowered scapes; these in cultivation generally revert to the one-flowered form.

The cups of the flowers in this species vary considerably in form; some being straight, very slightly crenulated, and not expanded; whereas in other flowers the cup is decidedly expanded, crenulated and distinctly lobed. I have compared these with plants collected by Mr Barr in Spain, and find that the latter are not so expanded as the ordinary Portuguese form, nor are the flowers so large; still, we often find plants here identical with the Spanish form."

In his catalogue for 1887 Peter Barr recalled hospitality received from Tait during a plant hunting expedition earlier that year and offered *N. cyclamineus* for sale by the dozen. In cultivation, *N. cyclamineus* prefers rather damp and acid soil and divides slowly. In favourable conditions such as at Wisley, *N. cyclamineus* will thrive and maintain its numbers from freely produced seed.

[1] Tait, A W (20 May 1886). *Notes on the Narcissi of Portugal*. Seven page note for private circulation. Oporto.

[2] Tait, A W (1889) Observations of Portuguese Narcissi. *Journal of the Royal Horticultural Society*, New Series XI:103- 106.

THE ENGLISH CONTRIBUTION

MALCOLM BRADBURY

Early Days.
The breeding of cyclamineus hybrids started shortly after the re-discovery of the species. Of these early hybrids 'Beryl' 6W-YYO (P D Williams pre 1907) and 'Minicycla' 6Y-Y (F H Chapman pre 1912) are still widely available. Bred from a division 9 cultivar 'Chaucer' crossed with *N. cyclamineus*, 'Beryl' suffers from the instability which often occurs when crosses involve flowers with different coloured perianths. 'Beryl' is at its best as a young flower when its perianth is a clear pale primrose. Unfortunately, as the flower ages the perianth becomes dirty, stained and off-white. As a show flower, 'Beryl' has mostly been confined to collection classes since the 1977 changes in the classification system obliged it to compete with cultivars with stronger cyclamineus characteristics. 'Minicycla' is a delightful miniature which flowers in late February and early March. Raised from *N. cyclamineus* × *N. asturiensis*, 'Minicycla' suffers from an identification problem. Over the years the cross has been repeated and I have seen cultivars ranging in height from 75mm (3in) to over 300mm (1ft), all claiming to be 'Minicycla'.

Leaving aside good garden plants such as 'Little Witch' (Mrs R O Backhouse pre 1921) and 'Bartley' 6Y-Y (J C Williams pre 1934), 'Pepys' 6W-Y (P D Williams pre 1927) is the only other early cultivar still seen occasionally at shows. Of classic cyclamineus form, 'Pepys' is rarely offered for sale and there must be a doubt about whether it is a "good doer".

The Breakthrough.
In *The Daffodil Yearbook 1940* the late Cyril Coleman, an amateur hybridizer from Kent wrote about his experience of growing what he called "Miniature Hybrids". He describes the 30 exciting seedlings which resulted from crossing 'Mitylene' 2W-Y (but of trumpet character) with *N. cyclamineus*. 'Charity May' 6Y-Y, 'Dove Wings' 6W-Y and 'Jenny' were named and introduced from this cross between 1943 and 1949. Not only did they dominate show classes for well over thirty years, they also inspired other hybridizers such as Grant Mitsch and Miss Verry to enter the field. Perhaps of equal importance, was their positive impact on the views of exhibitors about what exhibition flowers in division 6 "ought" to look like.

'Charity May', 'Dove Wings' and 'Jenny' flower in early to mid season ie a little later than more recent introductions. Healthy stock can still produce outstanding flowers, particularly of 'Charity May' and 'Jenny'. On opening 'Dove Wings' has an attractive almost luminous edge to its yellow cup, which unfortunately soon disappears. 'Jenny' has the strongest cyclamineus characteristics, but is a bicolour which only fades to all white late in the flower's life.

Cyril Coleman went on to explore the full range of form and poise available in division 6. Of these further introductions only 'Andalusia' 6Y-O is now widely grown and occasionally exhibited (see Fig. 10). Despite its strong cyclamineus characteristics I have reluctantly given up growing 'Andalusia' as it does not do well for me, despite growing well for other exhibitors.

Modern hybridizers
Though now closed, the Rosewarne Experimental Horticultural Station at Camborne in Cornwall raised several successful cyclamineus hybrids which were subsequently introduced by the trade.

Two of these have made a major impact on the showbench and others may do so when more widely available. 'Noss Mayo' 6W-Y (see Fig. 8) was bred from *N. cyclamineus* × 'Trousseau' and introduced by du Plessis Bros in 1986. At its best 'Noss Mayo' can hold its own with the more widely exhibited American and New Zealand cultivars. 'The Alliance' 6Y-Y was raised from *N. cyclamineus* × 'St Keverne' and introduced by Michael Jefferson-Brown. Though successful at shows, I found its corona bulky and awkwardly shaped and no longer grow it.

Ron Scamp continues to introduce a steady flow of first generation hybrids of his own raising. Of these 'Carclew' ('St Keverne' × *N. cyclamineus* 1993) has been successful at early shows and 'Crofty' ('Perimeter' × *N. cyclamineus*) will appeal to those who like its distinctive appearance (see Fig. 5).

In 1986 John Blanchard registered 'Swallowcliffe' 6Y-O. Raised from 'Cattistock' × *N. cyclamineus*. 'Swallowcliffe' has a short, but narrow and delicately shaped corona and in exhibition suffers from being a little smaller than other standard division 6 cultivars. As noted on page 20, John has also successfully shown a miniature cyclamineus hybrid of his own raising, but has yet to name it.

Michael Jefferson-Brown has registered division 6 cultivars of his own raising, but they have yet to be exhibited or introduced. Christine Skelmersdale has also successfully exhibited a miniature division 6 seedling of her own raising. Richard Brook, the raiser of 'Tripartite' 11aY-Y has exhibited a wide range of division 6 seedlings at Solihull and northern shows in recent years. At one time or another, I have seen an outstanding yellow self, yellow-red and yellow-pink seedlings. The problem here is that unless Richard registers and introduces them, his raisings will ultimately be lost to us. I have not discussed Alec Grey's introductions as this has been done by Delia Bankhead.

Overall, the English contribution is marked by a strong concentration on first generation hybrids and consequently on flowers where cyclamineus characteristics are clearly evident.

IRISH CYCLAMINEUS HYBRIDS

JANINE DOULTON

Despite being the world's leading hybridizers for many years, the Richardsons made little impact on division 6. 'Titania' (1958) and 'Joybell' (1969) are both rather large, show fewer cyclamineus characteristics than most exhibitors now prefer, and have had little success at shows. However 'Joybell' which has an attractive corona, thick waxy substance and a strong stem has proved to be a useful parent.

In 1986, Brian Duncan wrote to Rod Barwick on the subject of modern cyclamineus hybrids. Brian remarked that when he first became interested in daffodils in the early 1960s, 'Charity May', 'Dove Wings' and 'Jenny' were winning prizes everywhere, and that when looking at the records this was still true in 1984. He wondered how much progress has been made in this division since Cyril Coleman bred these three daffodils in the late 1940s. I think it would be quite safe to say that division 6 hybridizing, particularly in Northern Ireland has moved a long way since then mainly due to the efforts of Brian Duncan and Kate Reade.

Kate Reade's 'Foundling' ('Irish Rose' × 'Jenny' 1969) must be one of the best known blooms in this division. It is regularly seen on the show bench and continues to win many prizes. 'Foundling' has a deep pink corona and white perianth, the cup being quite short with short reflexing petals and a drooping poise. It is an excellent garden flower, sturdy and tolerant of most conditions and it sets seed well. My only reservation about 'Foundling' is that I do wonder whether it shows sufficient of the cyclamineus characteristics i.e. the really swept back narrow petals, to qualify for this division.

Having said that, 'Foundling' has been a parent for several blooms bred by Brian Duncan. 'Bilbo', 6W-GPP ('Roseworthy' × 'Foundling'), 1981, has a bright pink cup which is bell shaped and the perianth segments are wide and well reflexed. 'Delia', 6W-YWP ('Interim' × 'Aosta') × 'Foundling', 1984, has a pure white perianth and a soft pink corona. Although quite a vigorous plant it is rather taller than most division 6s. 'Elizabeth Ann' 6W-GWP (Duncan Seedling × 'Foundling'), 1983, is a favourite of mine, not least because it is such a pretty rimmed pink. The perianth is rounded and nicely reflexed and usually comes very smooth. I find this is one of the most consistent of the white-pinks in this division. It has won frequently at major shows during the 1990s for Brian Duncan. 'Georgie Girl' 6W-GYP ('Sputnik' × 'Foundling' 1989), has slightly unusual colouring, and has good poise. 'Kaydee' 6W-P ('Foundling' × 'Delta Wings' 1984), is a most consistent bloom with a very bright rosy pink cup and a pure white glistening perianth with wide perianth segments which are nicely reflexed. 'Reggae' 6W-GPP ('Roseworthy' × 'Foundling' 1981), blooms earlier than some division 6s which is useful for the show bench, and has a narrower cylindrical cup. It has a good form and poise more appropriate for this division than some other blooms.

Brian Duncan has also bred many other good blooms in this division, some showing more cyclamineus characteristics than others. 'Lilac Charm' 6W-GPP 'Roseworthy' × (R.562 × 'Rose Caprice' 1973), has become very popular with exhibitors and rightly so, in my opinion, because it is a little beauty with a glistening white perianth and a well shaped flanged trumpet which is lilac pink. The bloom is well proportioned and very refined besides being most consistent in shape and colour. Interestingly, it is difficult to see where the division 6 characteristics exhibited by 'Lilac Charm' and 'Lavender Lass' 6W-GPP, which comes from the same parents, come from. Brian Duncan, in his letter to Rod Barwick says that he tried without success to find the possible influence of *N. cyclamineus* in 'Roseworthy' which is in the breeding of both 'Lilac Charm' and 'Lavender Lass'. He considers that the reflexing form and small size may have come through from *N. poeticus recurvus* which appears several generations back in the pedigrees of both 'Rose of Tralee' and 'Wild Rose' which produced 'Roseworthy'.

'Delta Flight' 6W-W and 'Mary Lou' 6W-W are both bred from 'Lilac Charm' with 'Lavender Lass' as the other parent. 'Mary Lou' is a very neat bloom with a glistening perianth, but an expanded and serrated corona. 'Delta Flight' has also inherited a similar perianth but the corona is more bell shaped. Both blooms open with a hint of lilac or pink which fade to pure white quite quickly. Another 6W-W bred from 'Lilac Charm' but with 'Joybell' as the other parent is 'Sheer Joy' which was registered in 1992. One of my favourite blooms, 'Sheer Joy' has a well swept back perianth with overlapping segments and the trumpet has a rolled edge. It consistently produces good quality blooms for showing.

Looking at Brian's division 6 yellows, it is very interesting and encouraging to see that he has used *N. cyclamineus* in the breeding programme. It seems to me to be the most sensible way to maintain the cyclamineus qualities that this division needs. 'Elfin Gold' ('Golden Joy' × *N. cyclamineus* ?), 1983, is a golden yellow bloom of good substance which helps it stand the rigours of showing and has a bell shaped cup. A decade later we have 'Suzie Dee' and 'Suzie's Sister' both bred from 'Elfin Gold' × *N. cyclamineus*. They are both well proportioned blooms with nicely reflexed perianth segments, 'Suzie Dee' having a slightly expanded trumpet while 'Suzie's Sister' has a longer, straighter trumpet. Both have been consistent winners at major shows.

There are many other division 6 blooms that have been bred in Ireland but those I have mentioned are ones with which I am familiar and hopefully will encourage others to try growing them not only for showing but also for general use in the garden. I have found that most of the varieties mentioned have thrived in a raised bed with alpines and bring a good range of forms and colour in the Spring.

AMERICAN BRED CYCLAMINEUS CULTIVARS

DELIA BANKHEAD

Cyclamineus daffodils may be the most popular of the species hybrid divisions, and with good reason. In addition to their graceful form and endearing habit of being the first daffodils to bloom, their durability on the stem hardly has any equal. I have had blooms of many cyclamineus cultivars in good condition in the garden for as much as six weeks. Three of my favourites have been in bloom since early February, through snow, freezing rain and high winds, and still look reasonably fresh as I write this in mid-March.

American registrations of standard sized division 6 cultivars number 96, and 63 of these are the work of just one family. Many of the greatest division 6 cultivars had their beginnings in the fields of Grant Mitsch. He and his daughters, Elise Havens and Eileen Frey, are truly the First Family of the cyclamineus hybrids.

"Characteristics of N *cyclamineus* clearly evident..." was Grant Mitsch's motto when it came to naming new flowers in division 6, a practice carried on by his daughters. In a perusal of their pedigrees, one sees nearly every one has *N cyclamineus* at least once, and often twice in the last two generations of their ancestry.

All yellow.

In the all-yellows, 'Golden Years' is my choice for the best show flower, though it is not as strong a grower as the others. It is very similar in form and size to the wonderful Tasmanian cultivar, 'Abracadabra'. However, if I could grow only one cyclamineus cultivar, it would have to be 'Rapture'.(see Fig. 9) This flower is virtually unbeatable, in the garden, or on the show bench, as many years of show reports attest. Close behind it are 'Swift Arrow' and 'Warbler', which has a lovely green throat. They are a different style than 'Rapture', having broader perianths and uniformly flanged and frilled trumpets, in contrast to 'Rapture's straight one. Every bloom is show quality, and they are great performers in the garden. Other reliable winners are 'Skater's Waltz', a slightly smaller, very well formed flower with a hint of orange in the trumpet, 'Rival', (a little large for my taste) 'Perfect Spring' and 'Wings of Freedom', another slightly smaller flower.

Yellow perianth with coloured corona.

Any discussion of 6Y-O/Rs has to begin with 'Jetfire', old as it is (and supposedly virused, though it is certainly not in evidence in my region.) It is the most durable daffodil in my garden, and its substantial show record continues to mount, though its newer cousins are slowly overtaking it. Larger and more impressive, with more colour in perianth and trumpet, 'Straight Arrow', 'Velocity' and 'Arrowhead' are establishing records of their own. 'Arrowhead' and 'Velocity' have a distinct orange flush to their perianths. They are all strong growers, and make a great impact in the garden. 'Emperor's Waltz' is a charming slightly smaller flower with a shorter trumpet proportionately and is a regular show winner, as is 'Itzim', another old standby.(see Fig. 6)

Reversed bicolour.
Reversed bicolours seem to be made for division 6 - the swept-back petals show the contrast so dramatically, and the Mitsches currently have a monopoly on them. 'Swallow' and 'Wheatear' have long been my two best, for show and garden. Neither is totally consistent, but they both have good health, wonderful contrast and produce many show blooms. Oddly enough, if one has a bad year, the other is in great from, so growing both is strongly recommended. 'Lemon Silk' is a hauntingly beautiful pastel reverse with perfect form, but is not as strong a grower as I would wish. 'Inca' is a well-contrasted flower, which I no longer grow. Its proportions are a bit "Wagnerian" and it does not have as much reflex as I like. I suspect Elise's new 'Clavier' will become a champion as it becomes widely grown. It has all the attributes of one, and is one of the most graceful of the standard cultivars. If it proves fertile, it has the potential of breeding yellow-pinks, the colour of its seed parent. More reverses from this stable are on their way, notably UU2611 ('Glisten' × *N. cyclamineus*) (see Fig. 4) a very strongly coloured Y-W with great potential.

White perianth with yellow corona.
Three older Mitsch bicolours can hold their own anywhere, their only real competition being Miss Verry's beautiful 'Trena'. These are 'Perky', 'Phalarope' and 'Ibis'. The first two are very similar to each other, with unfading bright yellow gracefully formed trumpets and very swept-back perianths. 'Phalarope's trumpet is a hair longer, and both have a nice roll at the end. They are among the earliest to bloom, and are very long-lasting in the garden. 'Ibis' has a paler trumpet, and very good overlap to the nicely reflexed perianth. It is like a more refined 'Surfside', which is one of the largest of the Mitsch 6s, and too bulky looking for me. 'Ibis' also blooms later than the others, so is most useful for shows. Though they are more for garden than show, 'Sparrow' and 'White Caps' are also good flowers in this class. A new introduction for 1999 is 'Finite', which changes colour as it matures (in the manner of 'Sheer Joy'), and has been initially classified as 6W-Y. It has the typically elegant form that is the hallmark of this breeder, and I believe it will make a good show flower.

White perianth with pink corona.
The Mitsches have released very few pinks in this division. It is apparently much harder to meet their goal of true cyclamineus characteristics and get good pink colouring at the same time. Elise tells me she has made "massive" numbers of crosses in the last few years, so we can anticipate some good things to come. Two of their four registrations are seen regularly on the show bench, and win their share of ribbons. 'Carib' and 'Cotinga' have reasonably good reflex and lovely long trumpets, but the perianths are more ivory than white and the trumpets are on the peach-apricot side of true pink. Recently introduced 'Winter Waltz' is well worth growing for its earliness, grace and delicious pink colour. If there were shows in February, it would certainly win its share of prizes, too!

All white.
'Ocean Breeze' has led the field of Mitsch whites for years, but competition is creeping into the show reports. It is still my favourite, though its petals are a bit narrow, and its profile is wider than most. It is very white, and so reliable - every flower is of show quality. I have heard some comment that it is hard to keep going, but it has always grown well for me. 'Cazique' is of a different style - a larger flower with wider petals and somewhat less reflex. It has a stouter trumpet that opens pale yellow, and takes forever to whiten, but it is so long-lasting that it clears in time to win plenty of ribbons. 'Ouzel' is also a larger flower, built rather like 'Surfside', with quite a broad perianth and a bold look to it. One to keep in mind is the new 'Protocol', similar to 'Ocean Breeze', but with a more sharply reflexed perianth and an elegant trumpet.

Most of the cyclamineus cultivars of other growers are older flowers, and are not often seen in American shows today. One exception is the handiwork of Bill Pannill, whose three registrations are 'Durango', 'Cathedral Hill' and 'Magna Vista', all bred from 'Jenny'. 'Durango', 6W-W, is often seen in shows, and is his smallest flower. It does not reflex much naturally, but can be easily groomed. The newer 'Cathedral Hill', 6W-Y, and 'Magna Vista', 6W-W, are large, imposing flowers with great impact, which are beginning to be seen regularly in shows. They are very smooth, with great substance, and their broad perianths sweep back majestically.

Other colours.
Developments of other colours in division 6 have been slow in coming, but interesting things are appearing on the horizon now. Dr. John Reed has registered three yellow-pinks: 'First Born', 'Step Child' and 'Vickie Linn', and one white-orange, 'First Step'. I have seen only 'First Born', which, though not a classical cyclamineus flower, is certainly a good beginning. The most exciting new seedling I have seen is Elise Havens' T0611, a really striking 6W-O with a strong orange trumpet and broadly based perianth with medium reflex. Another of her seedlings of the same colouring, TEH 51/2, also has great potential. These, and the many recent introductions that are clearly advances in breeding, demonstrate plainly the Havens' continuing leadership in the field of American cyclamineus cultivars.

Tracing 'Trena' Territory in New Zealand

David Adams

After 'Hawera' New Zealand's second greatest contribution to the international daffodil and gardening world has to be Narcissus 'Trena'. This cultivar has won awards throughout the world and has been multiplied and marketed by the Dutch bulb growers. That such a flower should have unassuming beginnings is a story in itself.

Phil Phillips imported *N. cyclamineus* from Barr and Sons in the early 1950s. From the ensuing flowers he gave Mavis Verry one to be used as pollen. Mavis had been inspired by the British cultivars 'Jenny', 'Charity May' and 'Dove Wings' which were exhibited extensively.

Miss Verry used the pollen on 'Assini' 2W-W. 'Assini' was raised by W A Grace and registered in 1937. W A Grace became the first secretary of the New Zealand National Daffodil Society after being the catalyst for its formation. Miss Verry collected three seeds from the cross and thus were born, in the small rural town of Te Kuiti, 'Tracey', 'Trena' (see Fig. 11) and 'Tinkerbell'.

'Trena' has been the most successful exhibition flower and, indeed, created a sensation in 1986 when awarded Best Bloom in show at the North Island National. Never before had a flower outside of the first four divisions been given such an honour in New Zealand. It was interesting watching the judges gain the courage to fly in the face of accepted tradition. Most agreed that their decision was correct. 'Trena' was also judged Best Bloom in show at a National in 1990 and has seven divisional premier awards. 'Tracey' has four divisional premier awards and, whilst a lovely flower, 'Tinkerbell' is harder to grow and rarely seen.

Although Dr Thompson, famed raiser of 'Hawera', used the *N. cyclamineus* for crossing with other species in the 1930s it was not until the mid 1940s that cyclamineus hybrids began appearing at the National shows. The early catalogues do not list any division 6 cultivars. As with triandrus the non availability of the species inhibited progress in hybridizing.

The cyclamineus class was first included in schedules in 1935 but up to 1944 only three cultivars were exhibited. Cyclamineus hybrids became popular in the 1950s coinciding with the availability of the three British cultivars previously mentioned. A premier bloom award was first offered in the national schedule in 1976.

Phil Phillips' 'Backchat' 6Y-Y is still exhibited and Bob Spotts reports that it is useful for breeding.

David Bell raised 'Bonny Jean' 6W-W and 'Jeanette Gower' 6Y-Y. The latter has good form but lacks the refinement desired in cultivars in this division.

Others may already have said this but, at the risk of being repetitive, I present my view. Before being registered cyclamineus hybrids should clearly show the characteristics of the species. In my view 'Rapture' (see Fig. 9) fits this criteria completely. Many others only show two or three of the desired characteristics of the species. I suggest that short cupped cyclamineus hybrids do not fit the criteria and many do not have significant reflex. As a commercial grower I would love to have them reclassified as division 2 and then be available as top rate intermediates.

Max Hamilton initiated the recent development of cyclamineus hybrids in New Zealand. His 'Utiku' 6Y-Y ('Ristin' × *N. cyclamineus*) is a most consistent exhibition flower. It reflexes well and has good poise, rarely nicking the petals. 'Mangaweka' 6Y-Y is a smaller flower often with very long stems. By backcrossing the species on to 'Utiku' Max has a wonderful new 6Y-Y of good form and proportion.

Koanga Daffodils offer 'Red Socks' 6Y-R as a recent introduction. Whilst the deep yellow-red colouring of this flower is desirable the corona is very short.

Hokorawa Daffodils gained a premier bloom award at Wanganui in 1986 with 'Rufus'. This flower was most deeply coloured, almost 6O-O and was almost completely reflexed. There is now some confusion as a different form of 'Rufus' is being exhibited and has been reclassified as 2Y-R. The original form is still being exhibited thus adding to the confusion. A case of mistaken identity I fear.

John Hunter has used the species pollen extensively and reports a lovely 6W-WWP. He has some nice flowers from 'Arctic Gold' × *N. cyclamineus* with more to flower in the next two seasons.

Denise McQuarrie has used pollen in less traditional crosses and may have some interesting flowers shortly.

At the 1998 National show Graham Miller entered the six seedling class with a set of cyclamineus hybrids. They show great promise. Graham chose 'Loch Hope' and 'Drumrunie' as seed parents because of their smoothness and tendency to reflex naturally. The new hybrids demonstrate true cyclamineus character and have very smooth perianths. One has already gained a premier award. These flowers are most eye-catching with their drooping heads and slender orange coronas. Graham hopes to release the first of these on to the market in 2000. 'Jetsetter', with vivid red colour, has also been used as a seed parent but, although *N. cyclamineus* is the pollen parent, Graham will not consider registering the resulting cultivars as division 6 because they do not reflex significantly.

The late Alf Chappell had a wonderful set of miniature seedlings from 'Mitzy' × *N. cyclamineus*. The flowers were a perfect replica of the species and coloured Y-Y, W-Y and W-W. I fear that they are now lost. Colin Crotty used this cross as well. He has a fine set of pure white miniature cyclamineus hybrids.

My own 'Saturn Five' ('Gambas' × N. cyclamineus) has proved a show winner. Like a rocket ready for take off this cultivar is truly miniature in character. Bulb loss through fly and bad potting mix have not allowed greater availability. I have managed to retain only three bulbs. Fortunately there are that many in the USA.

We often think that members of the various daffodil societies are the only ones who hybridize the species. Members of the Alpine Garden Society have a lot of surprises. Val Robinson of Timaru has a plethora of high class miniature cyclamineus hybrids. Joe Cartman of Christchurch has a pot of *N. cyclamineus* × *N. triandrus triandrus*. Some have single flowers and others up to four florets of soft lemon colour. I wonder if any of these will ever become available.

I wish to acknowledge the work of John Hunter, NZ National Daffodil Society historian, for the hours he spent researching material for this article.

Cyclamineus Hybrids in Australia

Richard Perrignon

The production of *cyclamineus* hybrids in Australia has grown steadily over the last few decades. It can be divided into two distinct branches: miniatures and standards. Of the standards, perhaps the best known are Dr Temple-Smith's three seedlings bred from 'Ristin' × *N. cyclamineus*. In order of fame, they are 'Abracadabra', 'Voodoo' and 'Alacabam'. A full page picture of all three appears in the *1997-8 Yearbook*. Each is pure yellow, and combines the form of the species with the texture and, to some degree, the size of standard daffodils. 'Abracadabra' was registered in 1985. It must have the greatest show bench record of any division 6 in this country and it is also doing well abroad. It is characterised by its rich butter yellow colouring throughout, rich texture, rock-solid consistency, moderate size, and elegance of form. It is the embodiment of the hybridizer's dream: to inject some of the size and texture of standard daffodils into the hybrid without compromising the grace of the species. This, I believe, is the secret of its success.

'Voodoo' is very close in appearance, but its straighter trumpet is perhaps not quite as elegant. This has not harmed it, however, when it comes to the show bench, for its record is almost as enviable as its more famous brother. If it lacks anything in elegance, it more than makes up for it in vigour. In my experience, 'Voodoo' is the easier of the two to grow.

Like 'Voodoo', 'Alacabam' was registered in 1987. It is a little dumpy by comparison with its prodigal siblings, but full of personality nevertheless, and not without its own success on the show bench. All three are well worth growing for show.

For the crown of Australian breeding efforts, however, Dr. Temple-Smith faces intense competition from the mainland, where Fred Silcock has been busy producing 'Still Flight' (6Y-Y), and 'Perchance' (6W-P). 'Still Flight' is a long stemmed, pure yellow flower with a long thin trumpet and beautifully swept back petals. The flower is perhaps a little larger than Dr. Temple-Smith's examples, and its long stem may even suit it for the cut flower market. Its elegance is breathtaking. Like 'Abracadabra', it combines the texture and some of the size of standard daffodils while preserving the grace of the species itself.

'Perchance' is very different. As a pink division 6, it is probably without peer in Australia. Its Irish and American rivals, which often find their way onto the show bench here, seem to have no answer to it. Its long, thin trumpet is a solid, rich pink, and its petals are strongly reflexed, just like the species. Its flower size is smaller than 'Still Flight', but with a nice long stem for picking. Who knows what commercial uses there might be for this flower? It has taken line honours on each occasion that I have seen it exhibited, but alas, that has been all too rarely. Fred is one of the greatest breeders this country has ever seen, but as a perfectionist, he is often unwilling to release his beautiful work. If he does not, what will happen to it all?

The breeding of Australian miniatures in this division is undoubtedly led by Rod Barwick at Claremont in Tasmania. Every season he comes out with new treasures. Among the most fetching to date are the long-snouted 'Snook' 6Y-Y bred from *N. nevadensis* x *N. cyclamineus*. and his cheeky little 'Sassy', bred from *N. jonquilla stellaris* x *N. cyclamineus*. Though 'Sassy' shows clearly the form of the species with its swept back petals and long slender trumpet, its tendency to produce two flowers on occasion has relegated it to division 12 under RHS guidelines. Surely, a *cyclamineus* with six heads is still a *cyclamineus*! From *N*.

rupicola x *N. cyclamineus* Rod has bred four siblings, namely 'Mickey', 'Minnie', 'Mortie' and 'Ferdie'. Each is about the size of a generous thumbnail, and ravishingly beautiful. Rod's superb 'Swagger' 6W-W was bred from 'Gipsy Queen' × *N. cyclamineus*. Its slender white petals exhibit a Turk's cap reflex and its stems arch at maturity like its maternal parent. The trumpet is straight and narrow, opening greenish and maturing to white. There are many others, which space precludes me from discussing here. They include 'Slipp'ry' 6W-W, 'Nanty' 6Y-Y, the 'Glenbrook Mini-Cycla' grex, and the recently named 'Yella-Fella' 6Y-Y. All are worthy additions to the miniaturist's collection.

It remains to mention the up and coming work of Graham and Helen Fleming, of Keira Bulbs, Canberra. Their miniature division 6s, for the most part still under number, are usually exhibited at the Claremont Show in Tasmania in early September, and at the Bowral Show in mainland New South Wales in early October. All are tiny and exquisite, and exhibit an extraordinary range of form and personality. Their beautiful grex of 'Glenbrook Mini-Cycla' x *N. cyclamineus* has been released through Glenbrook, and it is hoped that many more of their creations will soon come to market. The breeding of division 6 hybrids in Australia is in full swing, and shows no sign of abatement This is a division to watch for the future.

The Miniature Cyclamineus Hybrids

Delia Bankhead

About 20 per cent of cultivars in the American Daffodil Society's *Approved List of Miniatures* are in division 6. Only four are not self-yellows, and these are all white.

All white.
'Mitzy', (Gray, 1955) is at the large end of the miniature scale. It opens with a yellow trumpet but quickly fades to just a shade darker than the creamy white perianth. It is larger and its petals are wider, better reflexed and a little more blunt than 'Snipe' (A M Wilson 1948). 'Snipe' is a lovely, delicate and very graceful thing, but its perianth is just too starry for a good show flower (which has not prevented it from winning many awards). The slender trumpet is a curious colour, with hints of pink, green and the palest of yellows as it ages to nearly white. 'Swagger', a recent introduction from Rod Barwick, is whiter than either and is quite a small flower with a slender trumpet and very good reflex. Its only drawback is a fairly weak stem. All are fertile, but because of its size and whiteness, 'Swagger' is probably the best to use for further breeding, and as 'Gipsy Queen' is one parent, it could produce reversed bicolours. One so rare it has hardly ever been seen is 'Dingle Dell' 6W-W, (P&G Phillips 1979) which aroused larceny in the hearts of all who saw it growing in Oregon. It is the finest white cyclamineus I have ever seen - pure white, with lots of substance, perfect form, size and poise - it was miles better than anything else available at the time. However by the time 'Dingle Dell' increases enough to allow its release, others may well have taken its place, as there is great activity in the Southern Hemisphere in breeding for white cyclamineus cultivars.

All-yellow
The tale of the yellows is bound to be a bit repetitious as there are so many of them to survey, but I will try to make as many distinctions between them as I can. As might be expected, all have good, clear yellow colour, so unless otherwise noted, this may be taken as read.

It often happens that some of the most beautiful are also some of the scarcest. My great favourites are 'Stella Turk' and 'Heidi', and one reason is their distinctiveness. 'Stella Turk', (Gray 1958) has the most beautiful waisted trumpet of any, and has, for my eye, the perfect balance between perianth and trumpet. It is also one of the latest blooming, another plus for me. 'Heidi', (Fowlds 1982) also has a beautifully shaped trumpet, and petals that shade slightly lighter and curve inward at their tips, like a Turk's cap. It has a very slender profile, like the species. 'Minicycla' (Chapman 1912) is another favourite, being quite small like the other two. It is a bit starry for ideal form, but has a most beautiful slender trumpet that expands slightly and has a very neat frill at the rim. It has a grace not many can match. There appears to be more than one form of this, the original 'Minicycla', but none should be confused with the grex Rod Barwick named 'Glenbrook Mini-Cycla group', which I have not attempted to describe. All these cultivars are rather finicky growers, and are not fast increasers.

Rod Barwick of Tasmania has registered quite a number of yellow cyclamineus cultivars, among them some of the smallest in the group. 'Ferdie', 'Mickey', 'Minnie' and 'Mortie' are all very small flowers, having been bred from *N. rupicola* x *N. cyclamineus*. I have not grown all these long enough to truly assess their value, but to date, 'Ferdie' is the best grower. It has reasonable reflex and a very nice lobed cup. Another one of minute proportions is Jim Wells' 'Totten Tot', a real charmer, like a smaller species, but hard to find. These five, with the three above, plus 'Little Star', and 'Swagger', I rate as the smallest of the cyclamineus miniatures.

Most of the rest are larger flowers and taller plants. One of the best is 'Hummingbird' (Mitsch 1975) with exceptionally deep colour and good poise. It has a wider profile than many, but good reflex, and is a very long lasting flower. 'Kibitzer' (Watrous 1964) and 'Mite' (Gore-Booth 1965) are a little too large for my taste, and not so graceful. Both have very narrow, pointed petals and a "hard-angled" look to them. Of Barwick's 'Nanty' and 'Snook', the latter is a better flower and grower. 'Nanty' has a paler perianth and less reflex. There are three fairly recent introductions by Americans which are all good flowers. 'First Kiss' (Link 1992) is a large, sturdy flower, 'Norwester' (Gripshover 1995) is smaller and has a pleasing form, and 'Spider' (Morrill 1979) has exceptionally clear, bright colour.

'Snook' and 'Spider' bloom earlier than any of the others, so are especially welcome in my garden.

Eileen Frey, a daughter of Grant Mitsch, has introduced six yellow cyclamineus recently. 'Bird Flight', 'Bird Music', 'Little Sunshine', 'Star Song' and 'Sunny Maiden' are all of the sturdier type of cyclamineus hybrids, rather similar to each other. 'Bird Music' has shorter petals in relation to its trumpet. 'Star Song' probably has the best form, is a deep, golden yellow and is a little later blooming. Two of these are coded 6Y-GYY, but I have not observed a lot of green at the bases of 'Bird Flight' or 'Sunny Maiden', which is in bloom as I write 10 February. The sixth introduction 'Little Star' is a much smaller and shorter plant. It has a light yellow perianth, with a deeper yellow in the outer two-thirds of the cup and with a nearly white halo at its base. The cup is slightly waisted and is flared at the rim. All these cultivars are too new to my garden to assess with assurance, but on brief observation, 'Little Star' and 'Star Song' appear to have the most potential. All seem to be good growers.

Two older flowers with little or no reflex are 'Opening Bid', one of the largest 6Y-Ys, bred by Alec Gray, and 'Zip', which resembles a better 'Small Talk' 1Y-Y, bred by Grant Mitsch. I think both would look more at home in division 1.

I have never seen four cultivars registered in this division - 'Atom', 'Flute', (I have acquired a bulb of this from New Zealand, but it has yet to bloom), 'Jetage' and 'Little Miss'. Some of these may be no longer grown anywhere and I would be glad of information concerning any of them. 'Jetage' and 'Little Miss' are the two with *N cyclamineus* as seed parent.

At the risk of being chastised by the Editor, I would like to include in this survey four cultivars whose cyclamineus ancestry is so very apparent, though they are classified as division 12. 'Cupid' and 'Flyaway' have been around a long time, though they may not be widely grown in the United Kingdom. Both are among the tiniest of miniatures, and can have as many as four delicate yellow classical cyclamineus florets to a stem. 'Flyaway' is slightly larger and better formed, with an overlapping perianth, and usually has 2-3 florets. 'Cupid' generally has more florets, and narrower petals. Both are simply entrancing little flowers, and though very finicky, are well worth the effort. They need exceptionally good drainage.

Two new division 12 cultivars with *N cyclamineus* in their parentage are set to burst upon the world scene. I believe they will become very popular, and in time, widely grown. Bill Dijk of New Zealand has newly registered his 'Little Becky' and 'Little Emma', both bred from *N. henriquesii* x *N. cyclamineus*. Usually with 2-3 florets to a stem, they are both very graceful flowers showing the best of both parents - beautiful cyclamineus form, but with trumpets that are indented at the base and lightly fluted and flared, with a scalloped rim (more evident on 'Little Becky', the smaller of the two.) They are as vigorous as their pollen parent, and are rapid increasers - in short, they are real winners, and I predict a great future for them, for show and garden.

There is great interest in breeding division 6 miniatures, in the USA and around the globe. In addition to Eileen Frey, who has more seedlings in the pipeline, Dr. Frank Galyon in Tennessee has a number of fine seedlings, including a good bicolour ('Ibis' × *N. cyclamineus*) and a beautiful reversed bicolour from 'Inca' × *N. cyclamineus*. Bill Pannill, Steve Vinisky, Helen Link, Mary Lou Gripshover, Leone Low and others have all shown very good cyclamineus seedlings in recent years.

But that's nothing compared to the doings in the Southern Hemisphere. There are no less than five hybridizers who have extensive breeding programs in division 6, and many seedlings (albeit mostly all whites or yellows) that have taken premier bloom awards. Rod Barwick and Kevin Crowe in Tasmania, and Helen and Graham Fleming on the Australian mainland are joined in a race to see who can produce the best new cyclamineus cultivars. In New Zealand, Bill Dijk and Colin Crotty are working just as diligently at the same goal. They keep the species going by collecting and planting seed every year, and given the size of their breeding programs, we can look forward to some major developments in cyclamineus cultivars from this corner of the world.

JUDGING CYCLAMINEUS HYBRIDS

JOHN BLANCHARD

Narcissus cyclamineus has one characteristic which is shared with only one other species, that is the almost complete absence of a tube (the part between the petals and the seed pod). In *N. cyclamineus* the tube is only 2-3mm long. Other characteristics which separate it from other members of the Pseudonarcissus Section are the bright green leaves (the rest are glaucous) and the smooth round stem. Other features are the petals which are reflexed by almost 90 degrees making them nearly parallel to the corona; the corona being "waisted", that is having a smaller diameter at the point where it begins to flare than at its base; and the deflexed poise, the axis of the flower being at an angle of less than 45 degrees to the stem. The petals and corona are the same shade of yellow, and the margin of the corona is dentate (toothed).

The definition of division 6 is "Characteristics of *N. cyclamineus* clearly evident: one flower to a stem, perianth segments significantly reflexed, flower at an acute angle to the stem, with a very short pedicel ("neck")". Clearly not all the features of the species will be found in most of the hybrids, and the definition requires only three of them. The "very short pedicel" is not strictly a characteristic of the species, in which it can be up to 10mm. The definition does not actually require that the cultivar should have *N. cyclamineus* as one of its ancestors, and there are doubts about whether all cultivars registered in division 6 have *N. cyclamineus* in their pedigree. However, judges should not enquire about the correctness of the registration. Any cultivar registered in division 6 should be judged as such. Judges must make their own decision when necessary about unregistered cultivars.

All the normal criteria apply when judging cyclamineus hybrids. It is unnecessary to comment on condition, texture, stem, presentation or uniformity (in vases containing more than one stem), except to say that a smooth round stem is not a requirement. These are standard matters to consider when judging all daffodils. Nor need much be said about colour. White and bicolour are as acceptable as yellow, with or without red, pink or orange in the corona.

Size (for the cultivar) does need to be considered. The *N. cyclamineus* parent or ancestor is a small flower, so the normal size for most division 6 flowers is smaller than one would expect for divisions 1-4. Great size is not to be preferred. One of the most important features judges should be looking for in all the division 5-9 hybrids is elegance. This is difficult to define but is obvious when you see it. Large cyclamineus hybrids tend to look coarse rather than elegant. However, that is not to say that smallness is a virtue. Most judges prefer not to award prizes to flowers which would qualify as intermediates or miniatures in classes for division 6 where no size is specified, though they are not ineligible. My comments apply equally to judging intermediate and miniatures in division 6, though the RHS and the Daffodil society do not provide separate classes for intermediates in that division.

When considering poise the definition of division 6 must always be borne in mind. In order to give it a "cyclamineus look" it is important that a flower should be deflexed, that is it should face below horizontal, or in common parlance for divisions 1-4 it should "hang its head". In division 6 it is a fault if a flower is horizontal or facing upwards.

Now we must consider form which, although in single bloom classes only carries 4 points out of 25, is usually the quality which decides the issue. In cyclamineus hybrids it is vital that the petals should reflex significantly. Many judges think it is better that they should also be convex and curve away from the corona rather than be plane or concave, that is curving towards the corona. Sometimes *N. cyclamineus* has twisted petals, sometimes untwisted. My preference in judging is for hybrids with untwisted petals, but others may disagree, and I prefer petals which are not too wide in relation to their length. If there is too much overlap, the flower can lack elegance. Many judges like to see the characteristic waist in the corona of long cup hybrids, but this is rarely so evident in shorter cups. The margin of the corona can be dentate (notched) as in the species, or entire (no notches). I feel that the former better shows the characteristics of the species, but that can only be if all other things are equal.

All these views are my own and not those of the Royal Horticultural Society or its Daffodil Show Schedule Committee, but I believe that my comments on registration accord with those of the International Registrar and members of the Narcissus Classification Advisory Committee.

Four Decades On

Frank Verge

Forty years ago I knew very little about daffodils or hybridizing, but on reading a book by the Rev Gourley-Thomas on the subject of hybridizing, I decided to experiment with daffodils. My first cross, which was supposed to produce a magnificent group of yellow-orange or red masterpieces, was 'Havelock' 2Y-Y and 'Fortune' 2Y-O. Needless to say, things did not quite work out as I expected. Out of 70 seedlings none showed any sign of red or orange or had a decent shape.

I began to realise that I needed better parents, so I bought a number of new varieties. In my ignorance I splashed pollen amongst these without much idea of what I was doing and flowered over a thousand seedlings from that year's crosses. I imagined that these new varieties, together with an increase in the number of seedlings, would automatically result in the production of some good quality treasures. But not a bit of it, not one was worth saving.

By this time I had learned two valuable lessons,

1. That great numbers of seedlings do not necessarily lead to success.
2. To be much more selective when choosing parents.

I was on the threshold of another lesson which was to take me some years to learn. I was advised by two very knowledgeable growers not to bother with crossing yellow trumpets as they could not really be improved. Also to leave the red cups alone as there were already too many of them. Unfortunately, with a few exceptions, I took this advice and regretted it. I do believe, when listening to advice, it is better to listen to those who express a positive DO, rather than those with a negative DO NOT. This said, perhaps that advice was a blessing in disguise, because from then on I concentrated on white and yellow bicolours.

By using varieties such as 'Ave', 'Empress of Ireland', 'Festivity', 'Newcastle' and 'Glacier', I bred some good bicolours and have registered 'Mereworth' 2W-Y, 'Ferryman' 1W-Y and probably, the best flower I have produced, 'Fiona MacKillop' 2W-Y (see Fig. 12), a large cup of trumpet character.

Apart from white and yellow bicolours, I have not concentrated on any particular breeding plan. I just tried to use good shapely flowers and left the rest to chance. I crossed 'Aircastle' and 'Mahmoud' which gave me quite a number of good division 3s. One very attractive one, which I named 'Shropshire Lass', has a white perianth with a narrow band of crimson around the lip of a yellow corona. Another, named 'Just Joan', which has a large white-orange cup, came from a random cross with 'Blarney'. Overall, I suppose I have bred about a dozen varieties that can hold their own on the showbench. Dotted around my garden are many seedlings that have appeared over the years. Though most would stand little chance in competition they are, like all flowers a pleasure to look at. It is a satisfying thought that they would not be there had I not had the inclination, years ago, to transfer a little pollen from one flower to another.

So summing up, I have no illusions of greatness about my efforts at hybridizing when compared with the great growers of the past and present. However I have had a lot of fun, achieved a modicum of success, learned a lot and made some marvellous friends. I would say to all growers, both young and old, have a go at producing seedlings. Who knows what might spring forth during the next four decades?

Breeding English Florists' Tulips - Our Genetic Heritage

John Wainwright

The English Florists' Tulip is a very special flower but relatively unknown today in comparison to its modern "Dutch" counterpart.

A long history.
The Florists' Tulip has been grown and bred in England for more than 200 years and the amazing flamed and feathered markings still fascinate so many people today. It was not until the 1930s that research overseen by Sir Daniel Hall at the John Innes Institute revealed that the "breaking" or "rectification" by which a previously single coloured tulip magically was transformed into one with beautiful stripes was caused by a virus. Until this point the apparent random breaking of flowers into good feathers and flames was a complete mystery, and the old growers had many weird and wonderful methods and theories on how this could be achieved. They also had very real problems of retaining un-virused stock, known as breeders, as just one aphid can easily transmit the infected sap from one tulip to another. Once infected the tulip and all its offset clones are permanently virused.

The English Florists' Tulip reached its height of popularity during the first half of the 19th Century when over 100 shows were held annually with many hundreds of varieties commonly grown and sold within the United Kingdom. A top show flower was much desired and would commonly fetch £100 to £200 per bulb, an enormous sum of money at that time. The reason for these high prices was that only one bulb in a thousand will produce a well marked broken flower after being infected by one of the Tulip Breaking Viruses; the other 999 flowers being rejected and destroyed or "ground under the heel".

Strict standards.
The early growers, known as florists, laid down very strict rules and standards to enable the beauty of one flower to be compared against another in competition. There are three colour types:-

Rose - Crimson or red body colour on a pure white base

Bybloemen - Lilac, blues, purples and slate colours on a pure white base

Bizarre - Browns, copper and reds on a pure yellow base

The **shape** of the flower is very important being approximately a half sphere when open to best show off the markings. This requires the six petals to be round and overlapping and equal in height. The **purity** of the base colour, either white or yellow, is paramount and in the breeder flower the size of the base is important. The stamens must have pure white or yellow filaments to match the base of the flower with dark brown or black anthers.

Gene pool.
Since the 1850s interest in the English Florists' Tulip has fluctuated and waned. Of the many hundreds of varieties that once existed, only about 30 good varieties of the English Florists' Tulip remain today in either the broken or breeder form. Little has been done to develop new varieties of the English Florists' Tulip since the 1930s, when Sir Daniel Hall was active, and most of the varieties now grown by enthusiasts date back to the 1850's and early 1900's. Once all the stock of a variety had broken then if it had not produced a well marked flower it was discarded however perfect its shape. Conversely, or even one might say perversely,

the two best shaped breeders, 'Goldfinder', a bizarre raised by Hepworth in the late 19th Century and 'Music' a bybloemen of similar age never produce well marked broken flowers. Most of the varieties which still exist today either as breeder and broken or only in broken form are not the perfect shape although all satisfy the requirement for purity. This however only presents a greater challenge to the few enthusiastic hybridizers today.

Because of the very intense interbreeding done by the old growers in the past in order to achieve "the perfect flower", the gene stock from many of the lost varieties is held locked away in the few varieties that we grow today, and recent interest in breeding from the old flowers has created some unexpected results.

After crossing, a tulip seed-pod swells to produce well over 100 individual seeds. Each seed produces a unique flower with its own distinct characteristics, but with genetic characteristics passed down from the two parent tulips.

One recent cross within the "Rose"' group revealed many flowers of varying quality and shape in several shades of red, crimson and pink. Many of the colours do not exist within the few varieties grown today, and could provide a valuable source for breeding and selection of new tulip varieties.

A recent cross using 'Bessie', another Hepworth variety from the last century, as both seed and pollen parent, produced seedlings falling into two very distinct groups of flowers. Possibly the seedlings reflect the qualities of the two grandparent bulbs last seen over 150 years ago when 'Bessie' was created. Of course it is not possible to extract exact replicas of the many lost flowers of the past, but it may be possible to regain many of the colours and qualities of the old flowers, now extinct, from today's remaining varieties.

The future.
The raising of tulips is not difficult but patience is needed, especially if the standards set down 150 years ago are not only to be maintained but also improved upon. It can take seven years to achieve a flower from seed and once a promising flower has been selected it may take a further five to ten years to build up a good stock. It will take another seven years for any back crosses on to parent flowers in attempts to intensify any desired characteristics. Careful lines of breeding and selection were the key to the early florists' success. Any flowers not meeting the very high standards set were rejected and destroyed. This must also apply today and any flowers showing impurity in base or filament colour need to be weeded out immediately. Breeding only within the three colour categories is preferred to accentuate the petal colour and to avoid bases which are not sparkling white or yellow.

Since the virus infection is not passed on through the seed, then all new seedlings should be virus-free breeders. These are very vigorous and multiply well so early selection of the best forms is essential if the number grown is to be kept down to a manageable size. It is hoped that during the next few years from the hybridizing work carried out by Peter and Beryl Royles and myself, 50 or more new varieties worthy of being named will be bred. They will all have to satisfy the rigorous standards laid down in the past and monitored by the Wakefield and North of England Tulip Society. Whether any of these will then break sufficiently well to win prizes as a broken flower is as explained above, purely a matter of chance.

We currently have only limited stocks of the English Florists' Tulip, but with a recent increase of interest in gardening and old flowers in particular, the possibilities for development of the tulip are unlimited. Today these flowers are conserved by a small group of enthusiasts with an interest in English tradition and of things historical and beautiful. The Dutch growers have been very successful in developing and maintaining the market for Dutch tulips over a long period. Maybe one day we might be able to combine the English Florists' eye for aesthetics with the Dutch commercial ability to make the English Florists' Tulip, in its breeder form at least, bloom once again.

Daffodils and Tulips in Latvia

Malcolm Bradbury

As the last of my daffodils died in early May, I was asked to make an unexpected business trip to Helsinki in Finland. Extending the trip by taking a few days leave made it possible to visit Jānis Rukšāns in Latvia.

Arriving in Helsinki on 22 May I noticed 'Ice Follies' planted in regimented beds in a city centre boulevard and 'Peeping Tom' in a park near the Sibelius Monument. The former had clearly been grown in pots and then planted out but 'Peeping Tom' had been naturalised. Next morning in Tallinn, Estonia I saw market stalls selling locally grown daffodils which I could not identify. Outside Tallinn the Silver Birch trees were only just coming into leaf. However as I travelled south on the five hour bus journey to Rigo more open tree foliage suggested that Spring was a little more advanced in Latvia.

On Monday 24 May I was met by Jānis who had driven 80km (50miles) to collect me. Jānis told me that the winter had been long and hard, with snow on the ground between late December and mid-April and temperatures as low as -30°C (-22°F). Cold weather the previous week had further delayed flowering, so there would be few daffodils and tulips to see.

Daffodils.
Jānis' nursery was surrounded by forest and on reaching the growing area I noticed the very deep peat mulch used to protect the bulbs. Outside the slatted and hence well ventilated packing shed I noted a clump of snowdrops still in flower. Few commercial stocks of daffodils had bloomed and even the early-flowering 'Jetfire' had only just opened. However, in the seedling beds there were some attractive bicoloured split-corona daffodils and cyclamineus hybrids which Jānis had raised. I was much too early to see 'My Angel' 11aW-YYW (see Fig. 15) or 'Freedom Stars' 11aW-YWW which Jānis bred from 'April Tears' × 'Canasta'. When making the cross, Jānis had pollinated 40 flowers, collected 17 seeds and waited nine years for the five survivors to flower. Except for some inevitable frost damage (see Fig. 17) all the daffodil foliage that I saw was very healthy. Jānis commented that eelworm was not a problem in Latvia as it died out within a couple of years; perhaps because of the very low temperatures. His only new pest was water-rats who dug up bulbs and ate them.

Tulips.
In the late 1970s Jānis started to breed tulips using *T. vvedenskyi* as a seed parent. His aim was to raise tulips which would grow well in his cool, wet conditions. Using a range of tulip species as pollen parents Jānis has selected and named several early flowering tulip cultivars. So early in fact that they were more numerous and colourful than the daffodils on the date of my visit. I was particularly attracted to 'Girlfriend' (*T. vvedenskyi* × T. *mogoltavica*) a distinctive early garden plant (see Fig. 19)

Other bulbous plants.
Jānis grows an enormous range of rare bulbs, many of them in carefully controlled conditions in polythene tunnels. Amongst them is the worlds' second largest collection of *corydalis*; the largest is at the Gothenburg Botanical Garden. Jānis is also well known for the many arduous plant hunting expeditions he has made to the mountains of Central Asia, collecting material for botanical and conservation purposes. In 1998 Jānis's last daffodil finished flowering on 28 June.

It was a unique and enjoyable experience to visit a most hospitable enthusiast whose growing conditions are so very different from those experienced by most readers of the *Yearbook*.

New Chromosome Counts in Narcissus Cultivars

Peter Brandham

The evolution of flowering plants is a subject that has fascinated scientists for many years. In the wild, new forms appear and old ones die out by a process of variation and natural selection that is well-documented but agonisingly slow in relation to our own lifetimes. The process of development and change in cultivation is much more rapid, because of the greatly enhanced levels of selection. Of course, this is not real evolution, but in some circumstances it can reflect the slower process that occurs in the wild, and is consequently a fruitful field of study. Cultivars of *Narcissus* are ideal subjects in which to examine the development of a decorative plant under the influence of mankind, because the genus has exploded in cultivation over the past 150 years from a few species and a small number of derived cultivars to the slightly larger number of species and the more than 25,000 cultivars that have been named from them. Many cultivars are now extinct, but the rest, which must all be propagated vegetatively as clones to maintain their identity, are of all ages and are ideal material for evolutionary studies, since the older and middle-aged ones comprise the intermediate steps that we can still follow today.

My own interest is in the chromosomes of these plants, and I have shown that the major pattern of chromosomal change in cultivation has been in the numbers of chromosome sets in them, i.e. their level of polyploidy. Most species and the early cultivars are diploid with two sets of seven (2n = 14), but later cultivars have more sets, with larger and more vigorous triploids (three sets; 2n = 21) arising from diploids probably in the 1840s, and even larger tetraploids (four sets; 2n = 28) arising from triploids in the 1890s.

Generally, diploid hybrids are reasonably fertile, except where the parents of the hybrid are very different in their chromosome structure, in which case meiosis in the hybrid fails and causes sterility (meiosis is the process of chromosomal pairing and separation that precedes the formation of pollen and egg cells, which normally have half the chromosome number of the plant producing them).

Triploids are highly sterile, because of their irregular meiosis, but they are nevertheless vital steps in the production of tetraploids. The occasional sex cell produced by a triploid avoids meiosis, it has the same number of chromosomes (three sets) as the plant that gave rise to it and is viable, unlike the remainder of the sex cells which contain an unsuccessful attempt to reduce the three sets by half and are not viable. In an appropriate cross, these unreduced triploid gametes will fuse with the single set of chromosomes in the sex cell of a diploid plant to produce a tetraploid seed with four sets. This will grow into a fertile plant that might be the starting point for further breeding. Plants with more than four sets are known, but are uncommon and I have suggested elsewhere that they are above the optimum level of polyploidy as far as size and vigour are concerned and are consequently not selected by breeders as being worth growing.

This article presents the results of my recent investigations on the chromosome numbers of *Narcissus* cultivars, most of which were not known previously, and discusses their significance. It is known from my earlier researches that most new *Narcissus* cultivars in divisions 1-3 are tetraploid with 2n = 28 chromosomes or thereabouts (since meiosis in these plants can produce viable sex cells with a range of chromosome numbers from 13 to 15, giving a potential viable range from 26 to 30 in the progeny). They are mostly fertile enough to be used in breeding programmes with a good chance of success, so it was not considered profitable to examine the chromosomes of many more of them, since little more significant information would be generated. Members of some other *Narcissus* divisions are at an earlier stage of chromosome evolution, because they comprise largely diploids and the triploids derived from them, with fertile tetraploids remaining uncommon or, in the case of division 5, unknown. It is of great importance to the daffodil breeders who are interested in these divisions to know the chromosomal constitution of their plants, because of the high frequency and low fertility of triploids and the need to adopt different techniques when using them in breeding programmes. The plants studied were therefore drawn largely from these other divisions, which have been found to be of greater interest as far as their chromosomes are concerned, or they were examined at the request of *Narcissus* breeders who had found that some varieties were unexpectedly sterile or unexpectedly fertile, or believed to be so. In these cases it was hoped that chromosome studies could shed some light on the degree of fertility or sterility of the plants.

Results

Chromosome numbers of 78 varieties were obtained from Feulgen-stained root-tip squashes and are listed in Table 1. A few of them (e.g. 'Lilac Charm', 'Roberta Watrous', 'Silver Bells') are confirmations of earlier results, but the rest are new. They will be discussed below under several headings, starting with chromosome number in ascending order.

2n = 14

These diploid hybrids would be expected to be reasonably fertile, with the exception of 'Elka', in which differences in the structure of the two sets of chromosomes indicate that the plant is a wide hybrid, i.e. the parents are genetically very dissimilar. This plant is unlikely to be fertile.

The 17 division 3 and 9 plants (poets and similar short-cup varieties) that were examined arrived with a claim that they had diploid seed parents. If this were so, they would be expected to be diploids or triploids, depending on the level of polyploidy of the pollen parent. Of these plants, seven were diploid as expected, but ten were tetraploid. Both parents of the latter would certainly be tetraploid rather than diploid, since tetraploid progeny from diploid / triploid crosses are very rare and difficult to obtain, so the information on the parentage of these plants is largely in error.

2n = 21

These triploid plants can originate in either of two ways. One is from solely diploid stock, with non-reduction during meiosis in one parent providing fourteen chromosomes and normal meiosis in the other providing seven. Triploids arising in this way are larger and more vigorous than their diploid siblings and are therefore often preferentially selected. In divisions 1-3 the first step towards polyploidy occurred via triploid formation over 150 years ago, but in some of the other divisions it is happening now (see below).

The other way in which triploids can arise is from a diploid / tetraploid cross. This will often happen when a cultivar (usually tetraploid) is crossed with a species (usually diploid).

Triploids are the cause of some confusion as far as their fertility and breeding potential are concerned. In the database of cultivars and their origins issued on CD-ROM by the American Daffodil Society, many cultivars known to be triploid are recorded as fertile, on the basis that there is at least one known record of their being a successful parent. This is misleading, since all triploids are in fact highly sterile. Meiosis in them is usually chaotic, with poor chromosome pairing followed by an unsuccessful attempt to divide an odd number of chromosome sets by two, resulting in widespread abortion of pollen and ovules. The only viable gametes that triploids can produce are those which are non-reduced and have the same chromosome number as the plants that gave rise to them. These non-reduced gametes give some chance of breeding success, particularly if the triploid is used as the male parent in a cross.

Although highly sterile, triploids are thus not totally sterile, although it is clearly incorrect to call them fertile. In *Narcissus*, absolute sterility can occur only in those division 4 varieties in which the double flowers have no functional anthers or stigmas.

2n = 22

These plants are triploids with an extra chromosome and come from tetraploid / diploid crosses with a chromosomal irregularity in the tetraploid parent. This uncommon chromosome number confirms that 'Suzie Dee' and 'Suzie's Sister' (both 2n = 22) are probably clonal, as suspected by their breeder, Brian Duncan, with one being a vegetative mutation or sport of the other.

'Silver Bells' was also found to have 2n = 22, agreeing with earlier records. This number fits the pedigree of at least one of the progeny of 'Silver Bells'. A very rare non-reduced gamete (22) from 'Silver Bells', fusing with a haploid gamete (7) from a normal diploid, has produced 'Lapwing' (tetraploid plus one = 29) and possibly others.

2n = 24

In most species and cultivars of *Narcissus* the basic chromosome number is × = 7, giving diploids with 2n = 14, triploids with 2n = ± 21 and abundant tetraploids (among the cultivars) with 2n = ± 28. In *N. tazetta* and its allies the basic number is × = 10 or 11, giving diploids with 2n = 20 or 22 and triploids with 2n = 30 or 33. Tetraploids with 2n = 40 or 44 are unknown. Members of the *N. tazetta* alliance can hybridize with the rest of the genus, but because of irregular pairing during meiosis the occurrence of 10 and 7 together in the hybrids makes them sterile, e.g. in varieties with 2n = 10 + 7 = 17, 2n = 10 + 7 + 7 = 24, or 2n = 10 + 10 + 7 = 27. The only exceptions are a few allotetraploids such as 'Matador', with 2n = 10 + 10 + 7 + 7 = 34. These have normal meiosis, since the chromosomes in one set of ten pair with those of the other set of ten and the two sets of seven do likewise. They are highly fertile and are proving to be excellent parents, e.g. of 'Falconet' and 'Hoopoe', which are both hybrids of 'Matador' and *N. jonquilla*.

'Explosion', 'Falconet' and 'Hoopoe' are sterile triploids with 2n = 24, and have *N. tazetta* chromosomes in them (2n = 10 + 7 + 7), in common with the well-known division 12 varieties 'Jumblie', 'Quince' and 'Tête-à-Tête'. Although sterile, they could be equally successful commercially, with their combination of vigour and multiple-flowered habit.

2n = 27, 28, 29

These plants are tetraploids with some variation in chromosome number (aneuploidy) resulting from meiotic irregularity in one or both parents, which does not always divide the 28 chromosomes into two equal groups of 14. Aneuploid sex cells with 13 or 15 chromosomes are sufficiently viable to survive into the progeny. Euploid (ie exact multiples of the basic number of chromosomes, in this case 7) and most aneuploid tetraploids are sufficiently fertile to be used in breeding programmes. An exception is in division 4, in which the double flowers often produce hardly any pollen because the stamens are converted largely or completely into petaloid structures. They frequently have no functional styles or stigmas either, and are thus completely sterile.

'Castanets' is an interesting unique plant. Its count of 2n = 27 is not (4 × 7) - 1 as in many other cases, but 10 + 10 + 7, which is the first record of this chromosome combination. Its probable chromosomal origin is 10 from one parent and 10 + 7 from the other. I would guess its ancestry as *N. tazetta* (2n = 20) crossed with a *tazetta* hybrid, either a very rare fertile one with 2n = 10 + 10 + 7 + 7 = 34 or a sterile diploid hybrid with 2n = 10 + 7 = 17 with meiotic non-reduction. Being an unbalanced allotriploid, 'Castanets' would be highly sterile, but in common with many other triploids it could see horticultural success through vegetative propagation. As it has 2 doses of *N. tazetta* chromosomes (2n = 10 + 10 + 7 = 27), rather than the single dose in 'Explosion', 'Falconet', 'Hoopoe', 'Jumblie', 'Quince' and 'Tête-à-Tête'(which have 2n = 10 + 7 + 7 = 24), it should resemble the *N. tazetta* alliance more closely than they do.

2n = 30

Two plants were found with this chromosome number. 'Interloper' is an aneuploid tetraploid with 2n = (4˜7) + 2, formed as above, as a result of meiotic irregularity in its parent(s), and it is presumably adequately fertile for breeding purposes. 'Soleil d'Or' (2n = 3 ˜ 10) is yet another example of a triploid. I have been working on the possibility that the names 'Soleil d'Or' and 'Grand Soleil d'Or' are not synonyms, but that two forms of this well-known cultivar might exist, a diploid with 2n = 2 ˜ 10 = 20 and a larger and more vigorous triploid with 2n = 3 ˜ 10 = 30, but so far no diploid has appeared. It still seems that the two names are used indiscriminately for the same plant, but the search for the diploid continues. If any reader can spare a small bulb of this variety, especially if it is long-established, I would be pleased to receive it in the continuing search for the elusive diploid.

B chromosomes

These are in several of the plants surveyed. They carry few genes, if any, and are transmitted erratically to the progeny. As far as breeding is concerned, they are neutral in their activity, having little or no effect on fertility, but conferring no advantages either. The highest ever record of their numbers in *Narcissus* was found here in triploid 'Martinette', which has three. The variety would be good material for teaching the occurrence and genetics of these largely parasitic chromosomes and its ancestors would also be worth investigating to determine their inheritance pattern.

Variable counts

Two chromosome chimeras were found:- The first of these, 'Dimple', has 14 chromosomes in most of the roots and is thus diploid, but one root had 28 chromosomes throughout and indicates the presence of a tetraploid sector in the plant. The variety has been reported to have breeding difficulties, which could result from the juxtaposition of diploid and tetraploid cells in the flower. Somatic doubling of chromosome number arising in this way is a regular but rarely-reported phenomenon, and can lead to the production of a sport if an entire offset is affected.

The other variety with chromosome number irregularities was 'Inca'. This is an aneuploid tetraploid with 27 chromosomes, but some cells with less than half of this number were seen. These were initially dismissed as broken cells which had lost some chromosomes during the preparation procedure, as happens frequently, but it was then noticed that they all had 13 chromosomes, and not a range of numbers as would be expected. A cell in this plant had unusually lost 14 of its chromosomes but kept growing and dividing to comprise a significant part of the cell complement. This is a very unusual occurrence, since chromosome loss usually results in early abortion of the affected cells. Again the juxtaposition of cells with 13 and 28 chromosomes could explain the reported breeding difficulties encountered in 'Inca'.

Divisions 5-7

These divisions, which include many miniatures, are attracting increasing interest among breeders. The chromosome numbers of a good sample of them are known and are shown in Table 2. I have often pointed out that the key to producing large numbers of vigorous, successful cultivars is to exploit polyploidy, as was done in divisions 1-3 (albeit unconsciously) when triploids appeared in the 1840s, with tetraploids arising from them in the 1890s. Triploids are sterile (see above), but are vital steps in tetraploid production. Table 2 shows that divisions 6 and 7 contain ample numbers of tetraploids, from which new cultivars can be raised with relative ease, but division 5 is another matter. Prior to the present work, division 5 was known to comprise only diploids and sterile triploids derived from them, i.e. it was at the stage of development occupied by divisions 1-3 during the second half of the nineteenth century. Now there is a major breakthrough. 'Lapwing' and 'Mission Bells' are tetraploid and are likely to be fertile. If they are crossed together, I am confident that they will release a host of vigorous fertile cultivars in this division for the first time.

Acknowledgements

I am grateful to John Blanchard, Malcolm Bradbury, Brian Duncan, Dan Du Plessis, Sir Frank Harrison, Sally Kington and Ron Scamp for providing the material for this study.

Table 1.
Chromosome numbers of 78 *Narcissus* cultivars

Cultivar	Division	Chromosome No. (2n)
'Akepa'	5W-P	21
'Androcles'	4W-W	28
'Atholl Palace'	4W-Y	27
'Bagatelle'	1Y-Y	14
'Ballykinler'	3W-GYR	27
'California Rose'	4W-P	27
'Castanets'	8Y-O	27
'Clare'	7Y-Y	14
'Cotinga'	6W-P	27
'Delta Flight'	6W-W	28
'Diatone'	4W-P	28
'Dimple'	9W-O	14/28
'Dorchester'	4W-P	28
'Dunkery'	4Y-O	28
'Elizabeth Ann'	6W-GWP	27
'Elka'	1W-W	14
'Explosion'	8Y-O	24+1B
'Eye Level'	9W-YYO	14
'Fairy Footsteps'	3W-GGW	14
'Fairy Glen'	3W-GWW	14
'Falconet'	8Y-R	24
'Fanad Head'	9W-GGR	14
'Favor Royal'	3W-GYR	28
'Georgie Girl'	6W-GYP	29
'Gresham'	4W-P	28
'Hill Head'	9W-GGR	14
'Hollypark'	3W-GYR	28
'Honey Bells'	5Y-Y	21
'Hoopoe'	8Y-O	24+0-1B
'Huon Pride'	4W-W	28
'Ice Wings'	5W-W	22
'Inca'	6YW-WWY	27/13
'Innovator'	4Y-O	28
'Interloper'	6W-O	30
'Intrigue'	7Y-W	21
'Jingle Bells'	5W-Y	21
'Joybell'	6W-Y	29
'Kiltonga'	2W-YYR	28
'Jamestown'	3W-GYY	28
'Kokopelli'	7Y-Y/Y	21
'Ladies Choice'	7W-W	28
'Lapwing'	5W-Y	29
'Lilac Charm'	6W-GPP	27
'Lincolnshire Double White'	4W-YYR	14
'Martinette'	7Y-O	21+3B
'Mary Lou'	6W-W	28
'Marzo'	7Y-Y	21
'Melbury'	2W-P	28
'Midget'	1Y-Y	14+1B
'Mission Bells'	5W-W	28+1B
'Mizzen Head'	9W-GYY	14
'Moon Jade'	3W-GWY	28
'Moon Tide'	3W-YOO	29
'Nether Barr'	2W-GRR	28
'Oryx'	7Y-W	21
'Parterre'	2W-Y	28
'Patois'	9W-GYR	14
'Port Patrick'	3W-GOR	29
'Prototype'	6Y-YPP	28
'Reggae'	6W-P	27
'Ringhaddy'	3W-GYO	28
'Roberta Watrous'	7Y-GYP	21
'Ruby Rose'	4W-R	27
'Satin Blanc'	7W-W	28
'Sheer Joy'	6W-W	28
'Silver Bells'	5W-W	22
'Soleil d'Or'	8Y-O	30
'Spalding Double White'	4W-YYR	14
'Sunday Chimes'	5W-W	21
'Sun Disc'	7Y-Y	14
'Suzie Dee'	6Y-Y	22
'Suzie's Sister'	6Y-Y	22
'Tamar Valley Double White'	4W-Y	14
'Top of the Hill'	3W-GYY	28
'Top Notch' × *N. jonquilla*	7Y-Y	21
'Torr Head'	9W-GYR	14
'Tracey'	6W-W	21.
'Whipcord'	7Y-O	21

Table 2. Records of chromosome numbers in *Narcissus* cultivar divisions 5, 6 and 7.
New or confirmed records are in italics.

Division 5	2n	Division 6	2n	Division 7	2n
'Akepa'	21	'Bartley'	21	'Aurelia'	21
'April Tears'	14	'Beryl'	21	'Baby Moon'	14
'Arish Mell'	21	'Bushtit'	21	'Baby Star'	14
'Auburn'	21	'Charity May'	21	'Bell Song'	21
'Celestial'	21	'Comet'	21	'Bobbysoxer'	22
concolor (triandrus)	14	*'Cotinga'*	*27*	'Bolton'	21
'Happy Easter'	21	'Cyclone'	28	'Bunting'	22
'Hawera'	14	*'Delta Flight'*	*28*	'Buttercup'	21
'Honey Bells'	*21*	'Delta Wings'	28	'Chérie'	21
'Horn of Plenty'	21	'Dove Wings'	21	*'Clare'*	*14*
'Ice Chimes'	22	*'Elizabeth Ann'*	*27*	'Cora Ann'	21
'Ice Wings'	*22*	'Elrond'	28	'Dickcissel'	21
'Jingle Bells'	*21*	'Fairy Wings'	14	'Divertimento'	21
'Johanna'	21	'February Gold'	21	'Eland'	21
'Lapwing'	*29*	'February Silver'	35	'Golden Incense'	21
'Lemon Heart'	21	'Foundling'	27	'Golden Perfection'	31
'Liberty Bells'	21	'Garden Princess'	28	'Golden Sceptre'	21
'Mission Bells'	*28+1B*	'Georgie Girl'	29	'Gripshover'	14
'Moonshine'	21	'Gimli'	27	'Hesla'	21
'Niveth'	21	'Golden Cycle'	21	'Hillstar'	28
'Rippling Waters'	21	'Golden Lacquer'	28	*'Intrigue'*	*21*
'Samba'	21	*'Inca'*	*27/13*	'Kokopelli'	21
'Shot Silk'	21	*'Interloper'*	*30*	*'Ladies Choice'*	*28*
'Silver Bells'	*22*	'Itzim'	21	'Lanarth'	21
'Sunday Chimes'	*21*	'Jack Snipe'	21	'Limequilla'	28
'Sydling'	21	'Jana'	21	'Lintie'	21
'Thalia'	21	'Jenny'	21	*'Martinette'*	*21+3B*
'Thoughtful'	21	'Jetfire'	21	*'Marzo'*	*21*
'Tresamble'	21	*'Joybell'*	*29*	'Mockingbird'	21
'Tuesday's Child'	21	'Larkelly'	36	'Ocean Spray'	21
'Ucluluet Gem'	21	'Larkwhistle'	21	'Orange Queen'	14
		'Lilac Charm'	27	'Oryx'	21
		'Little Witch'	21	'Parcpat'	21
		'March Sunshine'	21	'Penpol'	21
		'Mary Kate'	27	'Pink Step'	28
		'Mary Lou'	*28*	'Pipers Barn'	20
		'Minicycla'	14	'Pipit'	21
		'Nymphette'	27	'Polnesk'	21
		'Orange Glory'	28	'Porthchapel'	21
		'Peeping Tom'	21	'Quick Step'	28
		'Perfect Spring'	21	*'Roberta Watrous'*	*21*
		'Prototype'	*28*	'Satin Blanc'	28
		'Reggae'	*27*	'Shah'	28
		'Roger'	37	'Skylon'	22
		'Sextant'	28	'Snow Bunting'	21
		'Sheer Joy'	*28*	'Sugarbush'	21
		'Snoopie'	28	*'Sundial'*	*14*
		'Suzie Dee'	22	*'Sun Disc'*	*14*
		'Suzie's Sister'	22	'Suzy'	21
		'Tracey'	*21*	'Sweetness'	21
		'Trena'	21	'Sweet Pepper'	21
		'Urchin'	28	'Tittle-Tattle'	21
		'Woodcock'	29	*'Top Notch 'x N. jonquilla*	*21*
				'Trevithian'	21
				'Verdin'	21
				'Waterperry'	21
				'Whipcord'	*21*
				'Yellow Prize'	28

3 diploids	(9.7%)	2 diploids	(3.8%)	7 diploids	(12.1%)
26 triploids	(83.9%)	22 triploids	(41.5%)	42 triploids	(72.4%)
2 tetraploids	(6.4%)	26 tetraploids	(49.0%)	9 tetraploids	(15.5%)
		3 pentaploids	(5.7%)		
31 Total		53 Total		58 Total	

A Second Visit to the Hortus Bulborum

Wendy Akers

The timing of this year's visit to Holland to see tulips seemed to offer a better chance of catching the season. Last year it had been a hot and early spring and we only just managed to see the last day at the Hortus Bulborum and missed a lot of the Keukenhof tulips. This time we were seven days earlier and travelled from Hull to Rotterdam overnight driving off at eight in the morning feeling fresh not frazzled after a long drive through the tunnel. We arrived at the Keukenhof after torrential overnight rain and thunderstorms so it was interesting to see which blooms had stood up to this treatment. Several extensive plantings were all looking at their boots, others were completely untroubled and stood up strongly; 'Ballerina', a very elegant lily flowered tulip in orange and vermilion (one for a hot coloured pot, a hot-pot in fact) was standing tall, as was my favourite one from this visit - 'Barcelona' a very tall Triumph in a clear pink. 'Avignon' was another hot coloured one I loved. I see it is a sport of 'Renown' the huge pinky red single late that was at one time the only Dutch flower shown through the classes at the Wakefield tulip shows. For several years I was under the impression that exhibitors in the Dutch classes were forbidden to show anything else!

We had allowed more time for the Hortus Bulborum this year because I wanted to have a proper look at the Dutch breeder tulips. Over 250 varieties of breeder tulips were once grown in the 1920s and the Hortus still grows 43 varieties in blocks in alphabetical order. The oldest ones go back to 1863 down to the 1940s. The colours are extremely difficult to describe because they are so unusual, for instance 'Jaune d'oeuf' 1863 I described as "creamy yellow overlaid with peachy pink" but that doesn't really capture it. For 'Kathleen Truxton' 1942 I tried "pinky-cream with coppery-mustard and a yellow edge". I think that in the colour schemed gardens we have today they would be sensational. Walking through the breeders we became aware of a distinct and strong scent of roses and traced it to 'Orange King' 1903, in fact several orange varieties had this sweet scent.

The only other tulip I saw this year with a more unusual colour was in the hand of Anna Pavord at the Annual Show of English florists' tulips in Normanton. This flower was an unnamed seedling from Beryl and Peter Royles' breeding programme and it was a soft pigeon grey, quite beautiful. Anna had recognised it as "*gris de lin*" from the French "grey of flax" and to me it seemed proof that the genetic mix in the old florists' tulips is gradually appearing. *The Garden Book of Sir Thomas Hanmer*, originally written in 1659 and published in 1933 makes one realise that we have lost many of the seventeenth century words used to accurately describe colours. This is where I saw the word "grideline - flax-grey. From the French *gris de lin*". In his section on "tulipes - The Tulipe is the Queene of Bulbous plants." Sir Thomas Hanmer lists the various varieties by colour and has no hesitation in describing flowers as "browne purples" (anyone who grows 'James Wild' will know exactly what he means) and my favourite description "Ignatius, yellow and dead red".

Driving around Hillegom and Lisse in the sunshine and marvelling at the plantings of tulips in long strips of colour separated by canals is a delightful way to spend a few days in May and still refreshes me in retrospect in the hot dry days of July.

Obituary: Alan Hardy VMH

Alan Hardy, who died on 4 February at the age of 74, was for several decades one of the great names in the world of daffodil specialists and one of the most exacting judges. He was a leading figure in the great era of daffodil contests in the 1950s and 60s, when the Horticultural Halls at Westminster would be lined with massive exhibits from the virtuoso professional growers in support of each of the annual competitions.

Alan was not only a competitor himself then, but an aide of one of the most eminent growers of all time, J Lionel Richardson. During that era, tutored by Richardson, Alan was a daffodil hybridizer himself, entering with gusto the classes reserved for cultivars of the exhibitor's own raising.

Alan grew his blooms in the great walled kitchen garden of his parents' home, Sandling Park, near Hythe in Kent, which he later inherited. In cutting and preparing his blooms for show he was assisted by his wife Carolyn, whom he had met when she came there on a practical study course as a horticultural student at Wye College.

In the early 70s Alan retired from daffodil exhibiting in favour of Rhododendrons of which he grew several thousand species and cultivars in the huge Sandling woodland garden. But daffodils remained one of his abiding horticultural passions.

Alan joined the Narcissus and Tulip Committee of the Royal Horticultural Society in 1958 and remained a member until his death. For a number of years he was also a member of the *Daffodil and Tulip Yearbook* Committee. So keen was his eye for the finer points of an exhibition daffodil that he was often involved in selecting the Best Bloom at Westminster shows. He was meticulous in his fairness and had a reputation for giving as much attention to competitive entries of lesser

Alan Hardy with a favourite terrier in his garden at Sandling Park

quality as to those clearly in the lead. The Society acknowledged his services to the horticulture by awarding him its highest accolade the Victoria Medal of Honour.

So accomplished was Alan as a daffodil and rhododendron connoisseur that few who worked with him in these fields realised that they were only two facets of his horticultural erudition, his skill as a farmer and his knowledge as a naturalist. He had an intimate and vast acquaintanceship with trees and shrubs. He grew lilies, orchids and the rare primulas that almost defy cultivation. In company with Carolyn he grew chrysanthemums and innumerable half-hardy perennials. They grew vegetables and fruit both under glass and in the open. Theirs was a partnership of delight in everything that grows.

Fred Whitsey.

Daffodil and Tulip Notes

"Thomas' Virescent Daffodil", syn. The "Derwydd Daffodil"

Sally Kington

"Thomas' Virescent Daffodil" is named in part for T H Thomas, the 19th century Welsh naturalist who first drew attention to its singularity, and in part for the fact that the flower is often very green. The synonym "Derwydd Daffodil" is from the Derwydd estate, whose owner in 1906 wrote that it had been growing there in profusion for more than 200 years.

T H Thomas' find-spot is now swamped by the outskirts of Cardiff but Derwydd, 92Km (60 miles) further west, still has a colony, though depleted. The Countryside Council for Wales recently began to build up reports of churchyard sites across mid-Wales. Meanwhile, in the former grounds of Derwydd's near-neighbour, Middleton Hall, now the site of the National Botanic Garden of Wales, the daffodil has been found spreading up the field from a path along which it once seems to have been planted.

This is a double daffodil which in some respects resembles 'Telamonius Plenus', the 17th century daffodil still going strong in old gardens all over Great Britain. It is a single-headed, trumpet daffodil, with two or more whorls of petaloid segments arranged one outside and the other(s) inside the corona. The corona is sometimes entire, with one or more extra whorls of segments alternating with the petaloid segments within it, and sometimes more or less split to base and spreading open, with corona and petaloid segments spilling out (see Fig. 16). However, it differs from 'Telamonius Plenus' in certain significant ways, notably in the tube, which is broad funnel-shaped, and in the flower colour, which is more or less self-yellow. Many blooms have eight petaloid segments in the outer whorl. Its propensity to open and sometimes remain very heavily tinged with green might suggest a connection with 'Greenstar' 4G-G, but 'Greenstar' is a completely different shape. There is a closer resemblance to an unidentified, green-tinged daffodil from Newtonmore in Scotland (pers. comm. Reg Nicholl, 1993).

Peter Barr, who was sent "Thomas' Virescent Daffodil" a few years after Thomas found it, grew it on for comparison's sake. He suggested it was a double variant not of *N. pseudonarcissus*, as 'Telamonius Plenus' is thought to be, but of *N. obvallaris* (the "Tenby Daffodil"). Looking at it today, one can see his reasons. Into the bargain, he knew as well as we do, that the "Tenby Daffodil" is native to parts of the same South Wales coast that are haunted by Thomas' Virescent Daffodil.

In an informally combined operation, staff at the Botanic Garden at Middleton Hall and members of both the Countryside Council for Wales and the University of Wales Institute of Botanical Sciences, together with the Daffodil Registrar, aim:

To preserve the colony of "Thomas' Virescent Daffodil" at Middleton Hall.
To monitor its variation and spread.
To plot the whereabouts of other colonies
To note their range of variation.
To note what other daffodils are in the vicinity.
To collect samples from all locations,

including Middleton Hall.

To grow them all together in one or more "trial" grounds.

To grow other daffodils alongside "Thomas' Virescent Daffodil" for comparative purposes: eg, the "Tenby Daffodil"; *N. pseudonarcissus*; 'Telamonius Plenus'; other "green" daffodils, including those from Newtonmore.

To use DNA analysis and chromatography to discover any links between "Thomas' Virescent Daffodil" and other daffodils.

To examine colonies of the "Tenby Daffodil" for double variants.

To discover whether double variants resembling "Thomas' Virescent Daffodil" are reported in the wild in any other places in Europe, and if so, what other daffodils are in the vicinity.

References

- Stepney-Gulston, A., A contribution towards an account of the Narcissi of South Wales. In *Transactions of the Carmarthenshire Antiquarian Society and Field Club* (c.1906)

- Vachell, C.T., Contribution towards an account of the Narcissi of South Wales. In *Transactions of the Cardiff Naturalists' Society*, vol. xxvi, part ii, 1893-4

Narcissus x christopheri = *N. x koshinomurae*

JOHN BLANCHARD

Narcissus x christopheri was given a formal description in *Daffodils and Tulips 1997-8* as a wild hybrid between *N. assoanus* and *N. panizzianus*. Unfortunately, though I was not aware of it at the time, this plant had already been described by Fernandez Casas as *N. x koshinomurae*. He observed it at the very same location as I did at the Puerto de Encinas Borrachas in the Serrania de Ronda, but gave the parentage as *N. fernandesii x N. panizzianus*. I visited the site again on 24 February 1998 and on 22 February and 7 March 1999. On the first occasion there were a few *N. panizzianus* in flower but no sign of *N. assoanus*, but in 1999 there were flowers on both species though not in the same quantity as when we first went there in 1991. In 1999 there was just one clone of the hybrid in flower, tantalisingly out of reach. It was a much yellower form than the one illustrated in 1997-8, and the colour had darkened in the fortnight between though the form in cultivation has flowers which become paler as they age. I remain convinced that the jonquil species there is *N. assoanus* and not *N. fernandesii*. So the question arises as to which name has priority. Should it be *N. x koshinomurae* which was published first but shows the parents incorrectly? Or *N. x christopheri* which was published later but with the correct parents? I am indebted to Dr. Alan Leslie for explaining to me that according to the *International Code of Botanical Nomenclature 1994* the earlier name takes priority. He writes "... the application of a name is tied to the identity of its type. Therefore if the types of *N. x christopheri* and *N. x koshinomurae* represent the same taxon and *koshinomurae* is the earliest name, then it must be the correct name for that taxon, whatever opinion is held over its parentage".

So, sadly, the name *N. x christopheri* is invalid and must be discarded and, if a true *N. fernandesii* × *N. panizzianus* hybrid is ever found it will need a new name.

WHAT A DELIGHTFUL FLOWER

JOHN AND ELAINE INGAMELLS

Taking a holiday at short notice is often a matter of accepting what you are offered rather than the place of ones choice, which is why the 5 November 1998 saw us flying to Nerja on the Costa del Sol, Spain, a resort that we had never visited before.

Arriving on an extremely hot day we found

Daffodils and Tulips 1999-2000

Fig. 1: Narcissus *'1-29-86' 2Y-YYO was Best Bloom at the RHS Flower Show (see p.67)*

Fig. 2: N. aureus *was Best Miniature at the RHS Early Daffodil Competition (see p.65)*

Fig. 3: A vase of nine stems of T. *'Prinses Irene' which won the Walter Blom Trophy at the RHS Tulip Competition (see p.77)*

Daffodils and Tulips 1999-2000

Fig. 4 (above): 'UU2611', a strongly contrasted reversed bicolour Cyclamineus hybrid seedling (see p.27).
Fig. 5 (right): 'Crofty' bred by Ron Scamp from 'Perimeter x N. cyclamineus *(see pp.21 and 24)*

Fig. 6 (left): 'Itzim' (see p.26) and Fig. 7 (above) 'Jack Snipe', two division 6 cultivars which do well in the garden (see p.14)

Fig. 8: Bred at the Rosewarne Experimental Horticultural Station, 'Noss Mayo' has established a good record as a show flower (see p.13 and 24)

Fig. 9: The American bred 'Rapture' is a good garden plant and does well at early shows (see p.26)

Fig. 10: 'Andalusia' was bred by the late Cyril Coleman (see p.24)

Daffodils and Tulips 1999-2000

Fig. 11 (left): 'Trena', Best Bloom at the RHS Early Daffodil Competition (see p.65). Fig. 12 (above): 'Fiona Mackillop', an outstanding 2W-Y bred by Frank Verge (see p.35). Fig. 13: (below from left to right): Wim Lemmers, Jim Pearce, James Akers, Cees Breed, Brian Duncan, Sally Kington, John Blanchard and Ron Blom (see p.12)

Daffodils and Tulips 1999-2000

Fig. 14 (above): *A drift of snowdrops at Hodsock Priory near Worksop.*
Fig. 15 (left): *'My Angel', a multi-headed split corona daffodil bred by Jānis Rukšāns (see p. 38).*
Fig. 16 (below): *"Thomas' Virescent Daffodil" (see p. 47)*

Daffodils and Tulips 1999-2000

Fig. 17: Frost damage to daffodil foliage (see p.38)

Fig. 18: Jānis Rukšāns with his daffodils in Latvia (see p.38)

Fig. 19: 'Girlfriend' – a tulip cultivar bred by Jānis Rukšāns in Latvia (see p.38)

Fig. 20: 'Golden Oxford', 'Pink Impression' and 'Olympic Flame' in Derek Williams' winning entry for the inaugural Tulip Championship of Great Britain at the Harrogate Spring Show (see p. 85)

Fig. 21: 'Barcelona', a new AGM tulip (see p. 12)

Fig. 22: T. hageri *'Splendens' (see p.12)*

Daffodils and Tulips 1999-2000

Fig. 23 (left): James (Jim) Wells to whom the Peter Barr Memorial Cup was awarded this year (see p.51). Fig. 24 (above): Brian Duncan (left) presenting the Bowles Challenge Cup to Eddie Jarman (see p.68). Fig. 25 (below): The Rt Hon. Betty Boothroyd MP, Speaker of the House of Commons, holding a bunch of N. 'Madam Speaker' and talking to its breeder, Ron Scamp (see p.52)

that everywhere was very dry. There had been no rain for months and all the vegetation had the appearance of needing a good soaking.

In the area around Nerja, farmers grow their crops under extensive areas covered with polythene to create large greenhouses. The crops are flooded daily as water is channelled throughout the area.

Finding that there was not much to do in the resort, we purchased a booklet on walks around Nerja, one of which was to the disused Ermita de San Isidro. San Isidro is the patron saint of farm workers. Since 1986 a new chapel, in a different locality has been adopted.

On Tuesday 10 November we walked through the farmers fields to the old shrine which is two to three km to the west of Nerja. This area can only be reached on foot. No vehicular traffic is allowed except for access to the farmers plots. The area is very rocky and dry.

After climbing to the top of the hill we saw the Ermita. We had been led to believe that the area had an abundance of wild flowers, especially in March, but we were not sure what we would find in November. We had a quick look round the Ermita and then decided to try and locate any flowers.

On walking around the area we saw what could only be described as a miniature poeticus. It was the beautiful *N. serotinus*. To see it growing on top of a hill which was so barren was quite remarkable. There was no lush grass and no other plant life just stones and dusty dry soil.

There were only a few in bloom and they were all facing southwards towards the coast line. Most of the flowers had gone over and were showing good seed pods and other seed had already dispersed. However we thought the few remaining flowers were exquisite. The grey/green stems varied in height from 4cm to 10cm and the flowering plants were without leaf. The white petals which had no overlap were about 2.5cm (1in) in diameter and the corona was orange yellow. A couple of the flowers that were young and fresh had a distinctive green eye. There were three stamens slightly protruding but no stigma showing and the flowers had no noticeable scent. The seed pods were quite full.

As we walked we noticed that all the flowers rather than being scattered around were in a straight line, looking towards the west and Gibraltar and to the east Denia. Had we seen them a month earlier there would have been hundreds in bloom. From then on our holiday was spent walking around looking for more *N. serotinus* and hopefully *N. viridiflorus* but to no avail even travelling as far as Almunicar. Probably our visit in the Spring will produce jonquils and who knows what else.

WORLD DAFFODIL COUNCIL
BOB SPOTTS

On 24 April, 1998 in Belfast, representatives of the RHS and the national daffodil societies of England, Australia, New Zealand, and the United States met to discuss means to speed communication and increase coordination among societies on issues of mutual interest or concern. The decision was made that evening to form a World Daffodil Council with representatives from the various daffodil societies.
To date, the following organisations have agreed to participate on the Council:

American Daffodil Society
Daffodil and Tulip Committee of the RHS
The Daffodil Society
National Daffodil Association of Australia
National Daffodil Society of New Zealand
Northern Ireland Daffodil Group

The Koninklijke Algemeene Vereeniging voor Bloembollencultuur (KAVB) in Holland has also been invited. The International Daffodil Registrar for the Royal Horticultural Society will maintain an informational and consultative relationship.

It is anticipated that the Council will have two forms. First, an ongoing forum of communication among representatives using the Internet and electronic mail. To assure the continuity of communication, each organisation has two representatives, each with electronic-mail availability.

Representatives of each participating organisation will also meet at each World Convention. These representatives need not be the same persons as those on the Internet Council. However, the World Convention representatives must be cognisant of the actions of the Internet Council.

Numerous topics might be addressed by the Council. Among them: setting a standard structure for a World Daffodil Convention; award of future World Conventions; proper identification of miniature cultivars; international standards for miniatures and elfins (intermediates); common standards for judging "open classes" at World Daffodil Shows; promoting high standards for registration of daffodil cultivars; promoting daffodils in other countries such as Japan; encouraging international attendance at shows in all countries; sharing information on hybridizing advances and disease control.

It is intended that the World Daffodil Council will develop a Charter stating its goals, identifying its structure, and establishing its relationship with the participating societies. This Charter would be presented to the societies for approval.

THE RALPH B WHITE MEMORIAL MEDAL 1999

MALCOLM BRADBURY

The Ralph B White Memorial Medal is awarded annually or at the discretion of the Daffodil and Tulip Committee to the raiser of the "best new daffodil cultivar exhibited to the Society during the year".

In 1999 the Medal was awarded to Eddie Jarman (see Fig. 24) for 'Garden Party' 2W-WRR. Bred from 'Coral Light' × Bloomer seedling 352 ('Gem of Ulster' × 'Debbie Rose') 'Garden Party' was Best Bloom in Show at the RHS Late Daffodil Competition on 27-28 April (see page 73). As will be seen from the front cover 'Garden Party' is notable for the deep pinkish red colour in most of its corona. Such depth and clarity of colour adds to the growing evidence that daffodils with red coronas are more likely to be raised using pink cupped parents than by using descendants of the Richardson's famous 'Kilworth' × 'Arbar' cross which often pass on an unclear orange undertone to their seedlings.

Earlier winners of the medal were John Blanchard for 'Crevette' 8W-O in 1995 and Theo van der Hulst for 'Innovator' 4Y-O in 1997. The medal was not awarded in 1996 and 1998. Interestingly, all three winners of the medal are amateur hybridizers.

DAFFODILS ARE POISONOUS

MALCOLM BRADBURY

On 30 June 1999 newspapers in the United Kingdom reported the tragic case of Dennis Verity, 88, who became violently ill and died later in hospital from daffodil poisoning and malfunctioning of the heart. Mr Verity, who had poor eyesight and suffered from angina had accidentally cooked himself a meal of fried daffodil bulbs thinking they were onions.

Fortunately daffodil poisoning is a rare occurrence and deaths even rarer. Literature on poisonous plants* reports that the whole plant, particularly the bulb, contains toxic substances. Consumption of daffodil bulbs, leaves, stalks and flowers is said to lead to trembling and convulsions. Although death can occur, spontaneous recovery usually occurs within a few hours. Handling large numbers of bulbs and flowers can irritate the skin. Cases of daffodil poisoning usually either involve unusual circumstances such as the poisoning of cattle in the Netherlands, which were given bulbs to eat when feed was scarce during the war, or mistaken identity i.e. bulbs for onions, leaves for leeks and flowers and stems for a chinese vegetable.

*Cooper M. R. and Johnson A. W. (1984) *Poisonous Plants and Fungi in Britain; Animals and Human* Poisoning HMSO London ISBN 0-11-242981-5

Frohne D. and Pfander H. J. (1984) *A Colour Atlas of Poisonous Plants : a handbook for pharmacists, doctors, toxicologists and biologists* Wolfe Scientific Ltd London ISBN 0-7234-0839-4

THE PETER BARR MEMORIAL CUP AWARDED TO JAMES S WELLS

BRIAN DUNCAN

James S Wells, is this year's worthy recipient of the Peter Barr Memorial Cup. The cup is presented each year by the Royal Horticultural Society, on the recommendation of the Daffodil and Tulip Committee to someone who has made a significant contribution to daffodils on a national or international scale.

James (Jim) Wells (see Fig. 23) was born in England and spent many years as a nurseryman specialising in rhododendrons. He attended a meeting in 1951 of what subsequently became the International Plant Propagators Society and was its first president. Jim expanded the society nation-wide in the USA and subsequently in the United Kingdom, Australia and New Zealand. The society has now become truly international with a number of active regions in many parts of the world. A keystone of this work was his development of a new technique for the propagation of rhododendrons.

In his youth, Jim Wells had been introduced to the cultivation of daffodils in the early 1920s. However, it was not until his retirement some 20 years ago that he was able to develop this interest. Since then, he has focussed particularly on miniature daffodils, of which he assembled a comprehensive collection and has made a detailed study. Special interests include species in Section Bulbocodium and trying to resolve the ongoing confusion about the correct identity of many miniature daffodils in all divisions. In this work he developed a world wide correspondence with experts and himself became a recognised authority. Having in 1955 written an excellent book *Plant Propagation Practices*; The Nurseryman Publishing Co. Chicago 1955 (revised 1985), which is still in print, it is not surprising that he should later feel the urge to share his deep theoretical and practical knowledge of miniature daffodils by writing about them. *Modern Miniature Daffodils Species and Hybrids* was published in 1989 by the Timber Press (Portland) and in the United Kingdom by B T Batsford Ltd. This readable and well illustrated book is a worthy update and successor to the late Alec Gray's *Miniature Daffodils*; W H and L Collingridge London 1955. It is probably fair to say that Jim's book is the most complete guide to the identification and culture of miniature daffodils available and that it has contributed significantly to the growing popularity of miniature daffodils.

Jim Wells has two sons who are both associated with horticulture. His eldest son Roger is a land planner and uses his expertise and skill to guide large developments. His younger son Jeremy continues to run and expand the family business of growing hybrid rhododendrons which he distributes over the whole of the eastern half of the USA. It can be said that this is a truly horticultural family.

I had the pleasure of meeting Jim Wells at

the American Daffodil Society Convention at Calloway Gardens, Georgia in 1990 and was greatly impressed by his great good humour and enthusiasm. I was therefore saddened that he was unable to be present at the 1999 Convention in Pittsburgh to receive in person the framed picture of the cup and the plaudits of the audience of about 275 people. Instead, he arranged for Delia Bankhead to accept on his behalf and to express his appreciation.

'WHITE OWL'

SALLY KINGTON

There are two entries under 'White Owl' in the *International Daffodil Register and Classified List 1998:* One for a division 3 cultivar attributed to Barr and Sons; another for a division 8 cultivar of supposed New Zealand origin. The distinction between them, if there is one, is being investigated (bearing in mind that the present description of the division 3 cultivar is known to be wrong). Anyone growing a daffodil under the name 'White Owl', or with any other information that might help, should contact the Daffodil Registrar at the Royal Horticultural Society.

Note that the division 8 cultivar was originally listed as division 5 and was given as such in Peter Brandham's article "The future of Division 5 – Will history repeat itself?" in *Daffodils and Tulips 1998-9.*

MADAM SPEAKER

MALCOLM BRADBURY

In April 1998 The Rt Hon Betty Boothroyd MP, Speaker of the House of Commons, opened the Marie Curie Daffodil Collection at Harlow Carr Botanical Gardens, Harrogate. The Daffodil Garden was planted to celebrate the Centenary of the Daffodil Society and the Golden Jubilee of Marie Curie Cancer Care and is dedicated to the work of the Marie Curie Research Institute. To mark the occasion a new cultivar raised by Ron Scamp 'Madam Speaker' 4Y-O was named in her honour and planted in the garden. Unfortunately by the time of the opening ceremony 'Madam Speaker' had finished flowering. So on 16 March this year Ron visited Westminster to present a bunch of the daffodils to the Speaker (see Fig. 25). Bred from 'St Keverne' × 'Tamar Fire', 'Madam Speaker' is early flowering and sunproof

Book Reviews

Special Bulb Issue Quarterly Bulletin of the Alpine Garden Society September 1998. (pp 195)

This beautifully produced paperback includes 116 superb pictures of comparable quality to those in this *Yearbook*. Distributed without charge to then members of the Alpine Garden Society the *Special Bulb Issue* is available to non-members for £4.50 post free.* It is remarkable value for money and shows what can be achieved by a dedicated editor (Christopher Grey Wilson), a team of expert and enthusiastic contributors and the ability to spread high cost productions across a large print run.

Amongst the five general articles, three are likely to be of particular interest to *Yearbook* readers. "The Bulb Frame through the Year" by Dr Bob Wallis is a very practical "how to do it" article based on the author's experience of Access bulb frames. Growers of miniature daffodils and the smaller tulip species will find much to ponder in this useful contribution. "Showing Bulbs" by Kath Dryden reflects the Alpine Garden Society's tradition of exhibiting bulbs as growing plants in pots. Whilst standard sized daffodils and tulips do look contrived when exhibited in pots at local Spring Shows, I have often wondered why classes are not provided at major shows for miniature daffodils grown in pots. Lastly, "Bulb Literature" by Robert Rolfe is a comprehensive survey of the literature on dwarf bulbs. Readers who are frustrated by well illustrated but superficial coffee table books on general gardening will find more expert advice on dwarf bulbs well signposted by Robert Rolfe.

Contributions on specific bulbous plants cover Juno Irises, Hardy Orchids, the Genus *Erythronium*, Snowdrops, Daffodils, *Oxalis enneaphylla*, Crocus, *Iris winkleri* and Lilies. Despite a superb picture of *T. sprengeri* on the front cover, tulips are amongst the bulbous plants excluded from the *Special Bulb Issue* on the grounds that they have been "well covered in the *Bulletin* in previous years". "Some Superior Snowdrops" by John Grimshaw, Matt Bishop and Aaron Davies offers a well illustrated guide to some of the better *Galanthus* hybrids amongst the confusingly large selection now available. In "Narcissus Update" John Blanchard comments on the confusion caused by botanists and others amongst the shifting sands of *Narcissus* nomenclature and on some of the genuine difficulties of classifying wild daffodils. A final contribution of special interest to *Yearbook* readers is "Some Smaller daffodils" in which Christine Skelmersdale describes some of the more exciting small daffodil hybrids that make excellent plants for the garden.

Overall, the *Special Bulb Issue* strikes a good balance between in depth discussion of interest to enthusiasts and the width of coverage needed to encourage keen gardeners to grow something new. I strongly recommend the *Special Bulb Issue* to any bulb grower who has not already seen it.

Available from The Alpine Garden Society, AGS Centre, Avon Bank, Pershore, Worcestershire WR10 3JP

Malcolm Bradbury

Edited transcript of the Second Galanthus Gala, held at Bottisham Village College, Cambridge on 14 February 1998. £6.00 from J L Sharman, Monksilver Nursery, Oakington Road, Cottenham, Cambs CB4 8TW.

These events have quickly established themselves as a regular and well-supported part of the snowdrop season. The first was held in Cirencester in 1997 and the third this year in Worksop, Nottinghamshire. These edited transcripts enable one to experience some of the flavour of the occasion and thanks to the excellent colour illustrations to have a valuable record of a range of unusual snowdrops.

In this account Rod Leeds presents the histories of snowdrops with East Anglian connections. These include the late-flowering, little-known *Galanthus* 'Foxton', Sir Cedric Morris's *G. nivalis* 'Benton Magnet' and Kit Grey-Wilson's vigorous selection called 'Fenstead End' whose inner segments are almost completely a very dark green on their outer face.

In a talk which proved of great practical value Michael Baron covered some of the principal pests and diseases encountered by galanthophiles. The illustrations provide a clear guide to examples of Narcissus fly, eelworm infestation, Galanthus grey mould and garden swift moth all of which can deplete or decimate garden snowdrops.

Chris Brickell concludes the proceedings with a comparative account of early Bowles paintings of named cultivars in comparison with some of the plants we grow under these names today. He takes the opportunity to introduce the concept of standard specimens and the value they could have for gardeners. He also discusses two recently described Turkish species: *G. peshmenii* which is close to *G. reginae-olgae,* and the remarkably distinct *G. koenenianus* in which the backs of the convolute leaves are strongly ribbed - unlike any other snowdrop.

The transcript is presented loose leaf, with clear covers and a slip-on plastic spine. There is some evidence of rather rushed production as there is no title page (no title in fact) or date of publication, no pagination and no indication of venue or date of the meeting. The inclusion of all the discussion relating to domestic arrangements for the day may seem superfluous to some and there is a recurrent problem in which the words of the speaker refer to illustrations one cannot see. Ideally speakers might be asked to provide a written version of their presentations but this may be wishing for more than can reasonably be expected. For all those interested in snowdrops these transcripts will be a welcome addition to the steadily growing literature on a subject that for some is now an obsession!

Alan Leslie

The Tulip by Anna Pavord. Published by Bloomsbury Publishing Plc, London 1999, £30 (pp440).

"And while the tulip we extol,
We'll give the reason why;
'Tis not because their gaudy hues
Attract the vulgar eye, -
No! Tis because their varied charms,
As thus they brightly shine,
Remind us of the Almighty hand -
Omnipotence divine!"

This is one of the verses of "the poem written after the union of the Felton Florists Society with the Floral and Horticultural. It was sung at the second exhibition of the Felton Union of Florists and Horticulturists on 23 June 1845 to the tune of the hymn 'Of a' the airs the wind can blow'." It illustrates very clearly the way in which many people over the centuries, including this book's author, have revered the tulip. The reference also shows the detail which Anna has included in her book, the result of six years of research. It is a large book 24.5cm by 18.5cm (9½in × 7¼n) and almost 5cm (2in) thick, however it is set in a large type face which makes it very easy to read.

The first thing which strikes one when opening the book is the number and quality of the illustrations; almost every other page is a coloured illustration reproduced from museums and libraries throughout the world. If I have a small fault to pick then it is that there is no list of these illustrations which makes difficult the quick relocation of a particular favourite. The book is written in a style which is almost conversational and contains so much detail that I often found myself re-reading a chapter before going on to the next. It is therefore not a book which will be read in one session, or even two or three.

The book is not a practical guide to growing tulips in fact it contains no cultural instruction at all except when quoting old growers. There is a long introduction in which is related the author's own experience of first seeing tulips growing in the wild. "I knew how Galahad must have felt when he finally caught up with the Grail. At this moment I recognised an obsession that had been creeping up on me for some time. I suppose there must be one or two people in the world who chose not to like tulips, but such an aberration is scarcely credible."

The book is then divided into two parts. The first in seven chapters describes the history of the tulip from its origin in the East, introduction into Northern Europe in the 16th century and its development there particularly in Holland and Great Britain. "Now it had evolved into a hobby flower, but not before James Justice (1698-1763), Principal Clerk to the Court of Sessions in Edinburgh (and tulip maniac) had bankrupted himself in regular seventeenth-century style for the sake of his passion." Justice wrote "To make a soil...equal in goodness to this, for Hyacinths, Tulips, Ranunculus, and Anemonies and to make them blow and increase in the same way they do in Holland, is to most of our British Gardeners, a thing unknown." Does anything change?

Chapter IV "The Dutch and Tulipomania" is particularly fascinating beacuse it not only gives a full history of the phenomenon but also tries to explain why it happened in Holland; including the role played by America. Similarly the next chapter, "The English Florists' Tulip", brings to life the passions and rivalry, particularly between growers in the north and south, which this exhibition flower generated. Chapter VII "The Last Hundred Years" guides us through the creation in Europe and USA of the tulip industry, with the Netherlands now exporting at least two billion tulip bulbs a year. Here also is described how scientists set out to analyse exactly how the various colour overlays in tulip petals works.

The second part has only two chapters. Chapter VIII "Tulips: The Species", gives a very full description in a not too scientific way of each species. The wild location and growing details are given and often included is a brief anecdote from the collector. For example the notes on *T. edulis* (Baker) include "Siebold, who first gave this tulip its specific name, said that the Chinese and Japanese extracted starch from the bulbs of this species. They also roasted them and ate them like chestnuts."

The final chapter "Tulip Cultivars" gives the history of the naming of tulips, and a description of the current classification system. Here it examines the development of the various types of tulip and how as a characteristic became fixed, a new category was created. Thus at the end of the last century Messrs Krelage began to distribute Darwin tulips to distinguish them from the Cottage tulips which they resembled. In 1943 Darwin Hybrids were then introduced by D W Lefeber as a result of crossing Darwin tulips with species such as the brilliant *T. fosteriana*. The chapter ends with a list of commonly grown cultivars with a description of their flowers. A friend from Holland who had also read the book suggested that the list was a little out of date, but I would reject that since almost all the cultivars offered in the 1999 *Bloms Bulbs* catalogue are included.

The notes, bibliography and index are very comprehensive. There are references to 91 books and 30 periodicals, most of which I suspect have been read from cover to cover by the author. In her acknowlegements Anna writes, "Anyone writing about the tulip must acknowledge a great debt to Sir Daniel Hall, whose works *the Book of the Tulip (1927)* and *The Genus Tulipa (1942)* remain essential reading." As one who has waited for 50 years for someone to produce a book of equal stature to those of Sir Daniel Hall I can only commend this book to be read by anyone who has a love of flowers. Without doubt anyone writing such a book about tulips in 2099 will need to make the same acknowledgement to Anna Pavord.

James L Akers

Grant E. Mitsch Novelty Daffodils

SPECIALISTS IN HYBRIDISING
YELLOW-PINKS
SPECIES HYBRIDS
AND PINK-REDS

Mr. and Mrs. Richard Havens
P.O. Box 218A
Hubbard, Oregon 97032 U.S.A.

Many cultivars from Jackson's Daffodils from Tasmania also available – acclimated to the northern hemisphere.

***Colour Catalogue published annually
April - June***

U. S. $4.00 (airmail) for full catalogue
Visa and Mastercard accepted

Overseas Shows and News

Pittsburgh Someplace Special

Tony James

The National Show and Convention of the American Daffodil Society was held this year on 22-24 April in Pittsburgh, Pennsylvania. It was co-sponsored by the Daffodil and Hosta Society of Western Pennsylvania and the ADS Northeast Region. The three days of the convention were well filled with talks, garden visits, a riverboat cruise and evening banquets at which the guest speakers were the well known daffodil personalities, Spud Brogden and Brian Duncan. The whole thing was a "fun event", very well organised by an efficient and hard working committee.

The show itself was well supported and almost 2,500 flowers were on show together with about eight commercial displays. It was also something of a success for UK visitors. Brian Duncan won all three classes in the hybridizer's section. He won the ADS Challenge cup for twelve seedlings with 'Barnesgold', 1742 2W-P, 'Jackadee', 'Cape Point', 'Singin' Pub', 'Brindle Pink', 'Silverwood', 'Honeyorange', 91/30 3O-O, 'Lady Ann', 'Jake' and 'June Lake'. The flower of 'Jake' from this exhibit was outstanding and deservedly took the award for best bloom in the hybridizer's section. The Murray Evans Trophy for six seedlings was won with 'Gold Bond', 'Val d'Incles', 'Savoir Faire', 'Limbo', 'Dawn Run' and 'June Lake'. For the Goethe Link Medal, Brian used 'Ethereal Beauty', 'Dorchester' and 'June Lake'. It is perhaps interesting to note that of the 21 flowers exhibited by Brian in the three classes, ten of them had pink in the corona reflecting the interest shown by the American public in these flowers. In the open classes Brian Duncan won the Grant and Amy Mitsch trophy for the Best Vase of a standard seedling with 1789 11aW-P.

Brian's fellow countryman, Nial Watson, celebrated his first visit to an ADS convention by winning the Gold Ribbon for the Best Bloom in the show with 'Notre Dame' and his daughter Alice took the Junior Award with the same cultivar. Nial also had the best intermediate with a seedling of his own, 0033W, a perfectly formed 2Y-Y.

The Best Vase of three blooms was 'Homestead' 2W-W shown by Bill Pannill. This is a flower that should be seen much more frequently than it is, here in England, as it produces some very good flowers.

One of the major collection classes is for the Throckmorton Medal. Tom Throckmorton devised the colour coding for daffodils that we now use, and the class requires 15 stems of daffodils with 15 different colour classifications. American show rules require that exhibits be labelled with the cultivar classification as well as the cultivar name. I was a member of the judging team, which judged this particular class and it was noticed that the exhibit which was far and away the best exhibit, included 'Stratosphere' labelled 7Y-Y. This cultivar is variable and corona colour seems to depend on the climate in which it is grown. Indeed I have seen it win prizes at RHS shows in adjoining classes for both yellow and orange coloured coronas. Nevertheless it is registered 7Y-O, and this minor mistake by the exhibitor deprived them of an award. A flower from this particular exhibit was taken up for consideration for the best bloom award and made the last three from the initial twenty that were considered. That was the quality of the disqualified exhibit.

Reversed bicolours are very popular in ADS shows and there is a much wider range of cultivars shown. Perhaps none reach the standard of 'Altun Ha' but there are some very nice flowers and on this occasion the one to catch my eye was 'Swedish Fjord', a division 2 cultivar, raised by Grant Mitsch.

The classes for miniature daffodils in the show were very well supported and there are over thirty classes in the schedule including five collection classes, with one of them being for twelve stems. With this number of classes and the support they get from the exhibitors, it can be appreciated that the miniature section makes a big contribution to the show. The Best Bloom in this section was *N. triandrus* subsp. *pallidulus* shown by Steve Vinisky and the Best Vase of three was 'Stafford' 7Y-O, shown by Olivia Wellbourn.

The friendliness and hospitality of the American people at this event was outstanding and they all went out of their way to show that Pittsburgh is "Someplace Special".

AUSTRALIAN DAFFODIL SEASON 1998

RICHARD PERRIGNON

Shows.
1998 was a great year for Tasmanian shows. Hobart is usually one of the best, and on 5 September 1998, it did not disappoint. Rod Barwick took Grand Champion with his delectably smooth white trumpet, seedling 99/92. Mike Temple-Smith took Reserve Champion with his splendid yellow-pink cup, seedling 30/90. 'Langley Dandy' 3W-R, bred by the late Mrs. Murray, was the champion of its division, while Jacksons predictably took the championships for yellow and bicolour trumpets with their boldly formed seedlings, 1/91 and 95/91 respectively. One hopes these will be named and released shortly. Ian Norman's splendid white cup, 'Lady Diana', was the darling of her class, while 'Abracadabra' 6Y-Y notched up yet another championship for cyclamineus hybrids. Noteworthy blooms in divisions 5-12 included Kevin Crowe's double-headed, yellow tazetta seedling ('Matador' × 'Daydream'), his miniature division 5 seedling ('Silver Bells' × *N. triandrus* subsp. *triandrus*) and his pink-cupped triandrus bred from 'Decoy'. Rod showed an intriguing two headed bulbocodium, bred from *N. bulbocodium* × *N. triandrus*, and an exquisite bicoloured cyclamineus seedling, bred from *N. cyclamineus* × 'W P Milner'.

At Claremont, the results were rather different. Grand Champion went to the Radcliffes, with their now famous 'Redlands Too' 2Y-R. 'Abracadabra' was this time Reserve Champion, with Glenbrook's *N. scaberulus* as the champion miniature. 'Lady Diana' again took the championship for white large cups, while Rod's exquisite little 'Mortie' 6Y-Y was awarded champion of divisions 5-9, 10, 12-13.

Launceston is usually a later show, dominated by northern growers. However, Rod Barwick came north from Hobart to take Grand Champion, this time with his stunning white small cup, seedling no.57/94. In reserve, was Jackson's spectacular double, seedling 71/94. Geoff Temple-Smith took champion miniature with his beautiful example of 'Fairy Chimes'. Geoff is credited with passing on his love of daffodils to his son, Mike Temple-Smith, and therefore is a progenitor, in a way, of 'Abracadabra'. The Radcliffe's were deservedly awarded champion pink with their time-honoured Jacksons cultivar, 'Verran' 2W-P.

At Westbury on 13 September, the Broadfields' stunning pink seedling, 'Bella Donna', was the talk of the show. Other noteworthy blooms included Broadfields' boldly coloured 1 W-Y seedling bred from 'Flash Affair' × 'Calleva', and a broad petalled yellow trumpet seedling, bred from 'Dream Prince'.

Space this year does not permit a full review of the mainland shows. I must admit, however, that those I saw in New South Wales were perhaps not as glorious as previous years, no doubt due to the very dry season.

Overseas Shows and News

People.

Sadness came over the mainland in 1998 with the death of the well known and kindly Frank Coles of Mitcham in Melbourne. Many a cold Spring day did I spend with him in his five acre allotment, going through the many cultivars he had amassed over the years, much of it the work of older Australian breeders like Michael Spry and the Fairbairns. Lyla's hotpot would often pick us up over a lunch dominated by daffodil conversation, and one was always assured of a warm welcome at the Coles' place. Frank was well known for his tireless promotion of the record-breaking Olinda Show, and constant exhibition of daffodils over at least eight weeks every year in the Dandenong Mountains near his home. He had been President and Editor of the Australian Daffodil Society for many years. His passing is a sad loss to the daffodil scene in Australia, and our sympathies go out to Lyla. Another unfortunate development was Tony Davis' succumbing to a newly acquired allergy to certain plants, including daffodils, which culminated in a trip to hospital shortly after attending the Claremont Show. Tony has for many years been the mainstay of competitive daffodil growing in New South Wales and the Australian Capital Territory. Thankfully, recent information suggests improvement, but there will need to be, if serious competitive showing in his home State is to survive and grow.

Despite these events, preparation (largely thanks to Tony) ploughs ahead for the Australian Daffodil Championships, which will be held in Bowral in late September 1999. Visitors looking for a splendid show will not be disappointed.

NEW ZEALAND NATIONAL SHOWS 1998

Two very well organised National shows took place in New Zealand - one in Lower Hutt just north of the capital city, the other in Te Anau, a tourist centre amongst the mountains and lakes in the South Island - quite a contrast.

The season can be described in one word - ugly. Flower quality was not good and entries were down in both Nationals, although remarkably the Te Anau show in its isolated location was up to the usual norm in terms of blooms exhibited - close to 2,000 in all.

North Island.

Despite the general moaning open collection classes in the North Island were well supported, although the season hit the amateur growers with consequential lower than average entries.

Koanga Daffodils won the prestigious Class one with blooms mostly of their own raising. It fell well below their normal standard and only just beat the larger and more colourful flowers shown by IRN Associates. The same order presented itself in the class for British raised cultivars. A feature here though were blooms raised by contemporary British raisers in two numbered seedlings from George Tarry, 'Warbleton' (Burr), 'Uncle Duncan' (Pearson), 'Heamoor' (Scamp), and 'Desert Storm' (Postles). The entry was completed with the older varieties, 'Loch Lundie', 'Loch Loyal' and 'Golden Vale'.

The "Raised by Exhibitor" class was a close run affair - Brogden Daffodils regained the title from John Hunter with Graham Phillips a close third. The winning entry had excellent flowers of 'Centrefold' (still about the best NZ 3W-R), while 'Mt Cook' was an impressive new 1W-W.

The Yarrall Trophy is always the hardest to win - twelve cultivars one stem of each with no restrictions. Koanga were first from six other entries 'Cameo Sun', a very consistent 1Y-Y with classical form was very good in their entry, while 'Chaos' from Australia was also a fine flower. Peter Ramsay is producing many fine whites - 95:21, bred from 'White Glen' × 'Medici' was noted here

Prizes in the rest of the collection classes were well spread. The McQuarries made a rare trip North with many large, well grown flowers. Their winning entry in the class for nine yellow trumpets was glorious with 'Goldmark' outstanding. IRN Associates won the bicolours clearly from Graham and Faith Miller, but the latter won the red cup classes very clearly from Koanga and other aspirants. One of their own raising, 'Waitetei', looked to be an advance in the ranks of red trumpets, but was alas just short of the measure. Several prominent hybridizers were noted asking for pollen!

John McLennan staged an excellent set to win the Davenport Trophy, while the National President and his lady beat off twelve challengers to win the cyclamineus class - 'Trena', 'Rapture' and 'Willet' were the flowers. This is getting to be a habit.

The seedlings were not strong but as is always the case something new emerges. This time it was from the pollinating brush of Max Hamilton and was one of the best 2Y-P's yet seen. Smooth and well coloured it was some judges' choice for Best Bloom in Show.

As noted, Amateur entries were well down, but the season did not stop young Wanganui grower, Wayne Hughes from producing his best lot of flowers yet - six open class premiers no less! He did not enter the Waikato Tray and left the way open for John Hollever to have his name inscribed on the Silver alongside all of New Zealand's best growers. 'Egmont King' was a good flower in his entry. Ian Storrey was placed second with some great flowers of 'Cover Girl' and 'Evesham' but also included some rough ones too.

Wayne Hughes with quality blooms won most of the rest of the classes, but we noted Aussie-Kiwi Graeme Davis winning two collection classes including fittingly enough the one from his homeland.

Looking at the premier stand one was struck by the number of older varieties including 'Demand' (Graham Phillips), 'Bandit' (Spud Brogden), 'Trudie May', 'Centrefold' (both Wayne Hughes) and 'Highfield Beauty' (C and S Reid) appearing. There were four from the pollinating brush of John Hunter including a fine 'Polar Morn' (IRN Associates) and four also from the Koanga team including both doubles. We noted here 95:30 (Ramsay) which took best bloom at the National in Wairoa last year appearing again on the premier stand. It has a long way to go before matching the amazing record of 'Kiwi Magic', but it is very promising.

The Champion Amateur Bloom was 'Trudie May' (Wayne Hughes), and Children's Bloom 'Trena' (Natalie McFarlane - a thrill for her and granddad Don Stuart). The Best Bloom in show took little selection- a fine example of the Munro raised 'Snowy Morn', grown by Graham and Faith Miller. This was their first Best Bloom in show award at a National Show but will not be their last.

South Island.
On to the South Island where the local inhabitants were joined by a cabal of North Island growers lured by the promise of free and plentiful crayfish. It was served at the Dinner and went down well with Kiwi chardonnay. The show was marvellously supported by local people and a bus came from as far afield as Dunedin. Well organised by Malcolm Wheeler and the Te Anau Society the show was a credit to all concerned.

Koanga from North Island took Class one from David Adams of the South, thus exacting some revenge for rugby results. Do not mention rugby to anyone from Canterbury, but at the time of writing the Shield was still in the Waikato - please publish this quickly!

Spud Brogden got the double in the "Raised by Exhibitor" class with a nice set of flowers; beautifully staged as always. Koanga maintained their record in the class for twelve cultivars one stem of each, mostly with numbered seedlings. However 'Cryptic' a lovely pink raised by Jacksons of Tasmania was one of their best flowers. The McQuarries were second with 'Stormy Weather' and 'Tanya' the best of the bunch, and Ron Abernethy was third showing an ultra bright 'Kiwi Gossip'.

Ron triumphed in the class for yellow trumpets; 'David's Gold' standing out. In the second placed entry M and M Brown had a good 'Cameo Sun' which is proving to be very consistent.

Some of the other entries in the collection classes deserve mention; K and C Kerr from

Nelson put up a lovely set, including 'Badbury Rings' and 'Cool Crystal' to win the class for cultivars from division 3. Greg Inwood had a lovely entry to win the tazettas, and M and M Brown won the cyclamineus again. John Hunter beat Koanga and five other entries in the triandrus - all flowers in the first two entries were seedlings! However the outstanding collection came from the McQuarries in the nine whites - just beautiful with 'Florence Joy' and 'Cool Crystal' pristine.

David Adams had a delightful entry in the miniature championship. *N. bulbocodium* subsp. *bulbocodium* var. *conspicuus* and 'canaliculatus' were special!

In the amateur classes the battle raged fiercely. Sandra Muckle took the championship clearly with good vases of 'Red Cameo', 'Drumboe' and 'Dailmanach'. John Grant who travelled all the way from Dargaville - four flights plus car travel, was a close second. In the class for twelve cultivars one stem of each, Greg Inwood showed excellent 'Cameo Knight', 'Flying High' and 'Belzone', to head off young Aaron Russ who is going from strength to strength. 'Loch Loyal' and 'Matika' were good flowers. We were pleased to see Aaron (still at school) win two amateur class premiers with 'Silver Convention' and 'Homestead'. Well done, Aaron.

Robin Hill found the trip from Auckland worth while winning the class for six cultivars one stem of each, from five other entries. 'Grand Prospect' and 'Comal' were good in his entry. Don Stuart from North Island also won a trophy in the six Australian raised with a very tidy group.

In the classes for collections of three, local grower Malcolm Wheeler showed that not all of his time had been taken up with organising, by producing no less than eight winning entries. His real reward came though with Best Amateur bloom - 'Kiwi Magic'.

It was on the premier table that the McQuarries came into their own with nine very smooth and well-groomed examples. We particularly liked 'Tetherstones' for its bright orange rim. Premier children's bloom was taken by young Dunedin grower Ailsa Rollinson with 'Ethelred'.

Best Bloom in show was white for the sixth time in a row. However new names go on the roll of honour - Denise and Neil McQuarrie. The flower was a perfect example of the very consistent Brogden raised 'Florence Joy'.

So ended the season; one without many great flowers, but plenty of good ones. There will be lots of memories, but one of our lasting ones will be an entry which only won third place in the North Island seedling classes. Consisting of six new tazetta seedlings it was a great credit to our National Secretary and tazetta breeder, Wilf Hall. It deserved better!

RHS Show Dates 2000

Early Daffodil Competition	March 14-15
Daffodil Show	April 11-12
Late Daffodil Competition	April 25-26
Tulip Competition	April 25-26

All events will be held in the New Hall, Greycoat Street, Westminster, London SW1. For further information contact the Shows Department, The Royal Horticultural Society, Vincent Square, London SW1P 2PE. (Telephone 0171-6307422)

R.H.S. Gold Medal for Trade Displays
Engleheart Cup - 1985, 1986, 1990, 1993 and 1998
American Hybridisers Trophy - 1988, 1991, 1992, 1993 and 1999

Brian Duncan
Novelty and Exhibition Daffodils

Gold Medal quality bulbs
Direct from the Raiser

Consistent Exhibition and
Distinct Garden Daffodils
More than 300 varieties

Winners of many major awards
worldwide

For colour catalogue please send
U.S.A. $2.00 (Airmail) U.K. £1.00 (p.&p.)
to
Brian Duncan
"Knowehead", 15 Ballynahatty Road, Omagh
Co. Tyrone, N. Ireland BT78 1PN
Tel/Fax: 01662 242931
email: 113125.1005@compuserve.com

Snowdrops at Westminster

Alan Leslie

If the quality and variety of snowdrops seen at both the January and February RHS Westminster Flower Shows is any guide, interest in this genus continues at fever-pitch. Several new publications are known to be in the offing and there is renewed interest in studying the wild populations which, in many cases, are still surprisingly poorly understood and recorded. Every season sees a crop of new cultivars, some of which will be good garden plants and they include enough oddities to please all tastes.

January brought two snowdrops of note before the Joint Rock Garden Plant Committee. *Galanthus plicatus* 'Florence Baker' impressed the Committee as an early flowering plicate snowdrop with exceptionally broad leaves and strong, tall stems. The single flowers bear an X-shaped mark on the inner segments, the basal arms of the × being very much paler. Found in a garden population at Owletts in Kent, it deserved its Certificate of Preliminary Commendation and was exhibited by Dr Ronald Mackenzie. At the same meeting, John Blanchard exhibited, for interest, plants derived from a collection made in the Sierra de Gudar, east of Madrid. That snowdrops grow wild in Spain at all comes as a surprise to many and their identity continues to pose problems. Traditionally recorded as *G. nivalis,* they may well be related to similar populations in parts of Italy and, perhaps, also in the Balkans. They may best be placed in *G. reginae-olgae* subsp. *vernalis* but more work is required to sort out their relationship to G. *nivalis.*

January, though, was merely a taster for the spectacle of the February Show. Foxgrove, in particular, devoted the whole of their Gold Medal stand to a superbly presented collection of snowdrops. Shown against a bed of fresh green moss, they included plants of the true 'Mighty Atom', whose large flowers are borne on short stems and whose inner petal mark is very precisely defined and of the deepest green. 'Blond Inge' is a delicate little G. *nivalis* selection, found in a German graveyard and unique in the inner petal marking being yellow whilst the ovary is the normal green. Many also lost their heart to 'Trym', a distinctive snowdrop if ever there was one, in which the outer segments are like slightly larger versions of the inners and with the similar bold, V-shaped mark on the outer face. The name derives from Westbury-on-Trym, in Bristol, where it was found in a garden in the 1970s. Rather slow to increase, it is only now starting to "get around".

Another remarkable set of snowdrops came down to the dais after exhibition before Joint Rock. Although not at its best on the day, the star turn here must be what is now christened *G. elwesii* 'Joy Cozens'. Discovered in a Gloucestershire garden and exhibited by Mrs Mary Strood, the flowers are distinctly suffused a pale, almost orange-tinted cream whilst in bud and for the first few days after opening. They then fade to white but darken again if the flowers are pressed and dried. There are nineteenth century records of pink-flowered snowdrops, largely dismissed as nonsense, but this discovery raises the interesting possibility that such a thing could have occurred and who knows what seedlings of 'Joy Cozens' might produce!

Dr Mackenzie also exhibited again, showing no less than seven magnificent clumps of snowdrops in huge (and very heavy) clay pots. No-one does it better! They included the true 'Colesbourne', which combines a short stem, grey convolute foliage and distinctive flowers, with their long, narrow ovary and almost solid green inner segments; there are impostors around under this name. The pan of 'Cowhouse Green' (with the *outers* strongly suffused with green) made the galanthophiles swoon but left the Committee cold; but they did fall for 'Bill Bishop', another relatively short-stemmed but large-flowered snowdrop. It has long arching pedicels which sometimes carry the flower almost down to ground level. Both the latter and the neat, old Irish double 'Hill Poë' were recommended as candidates for the Award of Garden Merit (AGM).

Last but not least amongst this feast of snowdrops was a large and vigorous clone of 'Sandersii', the form of *G. nivalis* with yellow marks and yellow ovaries. These always cause comment and are eagerly sought after - at a price! However they have a reputation for being slow and difficult in cultivation, which may be due to an unrecognised and uncharacteristic preference for a more acid loam than other snowdrops. This particular clone had shown itself more vigorous a garden plant and was as large a "yellow" as most had seen before. John Foster, who exhibited it, proposes to call it 'Ray Cobb'.

THE DAFFODIL SOCIETY
(Founded 1898)

THE SPECIALIST SOCIETY FOR ALL DAFFODIL ENTHUSIASTS

Providing companionship, shared knowledge and advice, and information on growing and showing technique for over 100 years. Please join us.

**Details from the Secretary:
Mrs Jackie Petherbridge, The Meadows, Puxton, North Somerset BS24 6TF**

RHS Early Daffodil Competition

John Goddard

After the magnificent display last year because of the early season, I suppose that this show on 16-17 March could be described as disappointing. However, the 172 stems on display from 9 exhibitors included some quality flowers. A varied range of good seedlings also attracted the interest of both experts and the general public.

Collection classes.
The class for six cultivars from any division was won by Dan du Plessis. Although he has won this class before, he was particularly delighted with this entry which included 'Osmington', 'Hero', 'Sealing Wax', 'Chief Inspector', 'Canisp' and 'Knightsbridge' - a good mix of colours and divisions. Second was Ron Scamp who had Reserve Best Bloom in show with 'Trumpet Warrior' 1YYW-WWY. I also liked his 'Kiwi Sunset' and 'Madam Speaker'. John Gibson was third with some very promising seedlings under number. In class 2, John Gibson had a superb seedling 3-6-89 2Y-R in his winning entry in class 2. In his second placed entry Ron Scamp showed an excellent vase of three 'Kiwi Sunset' which gave rise to a lot of favourable comments.

The last of the collection classes called for three vases of three division 6 cultivars and here Ron Scamp and Dan du Plessis reigned supreme with both showing excellent vases of 'Rapture' and 'Trena' with Ron also using 'Warbler' and Dan 'The Alliance'. J M Parkinson also used the first two cultivars plus 'Charity May' to come third.

Single bloom classes.
Amongst the single bloom classes Reg Nicholl won with 'Bega' 1Y-Y which I had not seen before. It had the good colour and flat perianth typical of many of Jackson's raisings from Tasmania. Other flowers of note were 'Helford Dawn' from Dan and John Gibson's 1-16-92 3W-W, which flowers very early for this type of cultivar. We had two more seedlings, S890 4W-P and 46/25 4Y-Y from Ron and Dan respectively but the Best Bloom in show was Ron's 'Trena' 6W-Y (see Fig. 11). What a superb bloom this was, a lovely colour and a broad glistening perianth.

John Blanchard dominated the miniature classes and was awarded Best Miniature with *N. aureus* (see Fig. 2). For myself, however, I still drool over his 'Crevette' which again won the class for hybrid miniature daffodils. There will be a scramble if this is ever released commercially in the United Kingdom.

One good thing to emerge from this early show was the interest shown by the general public who seemed to be more numerous this year. When one looks back on the beginnings of this venture it must be most gratifying to those who had the courage to see it through after a more than tentative start.

SHOW RESULTS

Peter Wilkins

The number in brackets denotes the number of entries staged in the class.

Class 1: Six cultivars, one stem of each, any division or divisions (5). 1. D du Plessis: Osmington, Hero, Sealing Wax, Chief Inspector, Canisp, Knightsbridge. 2. R Scamp: Trumpet Warrior (Reserve Best Bloom), Helford Dawn, S888, Kiwi Sunset, Madam Speaker, Gwinear. 3. S Gibson: 1-22-92, Gin & Lime, A-6-91, 1-20-92, 1-1-92, Ballyrobert.

Class 2: Three cultivars, three stems of each, any division or divisions (3). 1. S Gibson: Michaels Gold, 3-6-89, B-6-91. 2. R Scamp: Helford Dawn, Kiwi Sunset, S113. 3. D du Plessis: Sealing Wax, Avalanche, Sportsman.

Class 3: Three cultivars, division 6, three blooms of each (4).
1. R Scamp: Rapture, Trena, Warbler. 2. D du Plessis: Rapture, Trena, The Alliance. 3. J Parkinson: Rapture, Trena, Charity May.

Class 4: One bloom, division 1 (8). 1. R Nicholl: Bega. 2. M Baxter: Tenterfield. 3. J Parkinson: Ristin.

Class 5: One bloom, division 2 (5). 1. D du Plessis: Helford Dawn. 2. R Wiseman: Vahu. 3. J Parkinson: Michaels Gold.

Class 6: One bloom, division 3 (3). 1. S Gibson: 1-16-92. 2. D du Plessis: Park Springs. 3. R Scamp: Doubtful.

Class 7: One bloom, division 4 (3). 1. R Scamp: S890. 2. D du Plessis: 46/25. 3. R Wiseman: Tamar Fire.

Class 8: One bloom, division 6, yellow perianth (6). 1. R Wiseman: Lemon Silk. 2. M Baxter: Warbler. 3. R Nicholl: Rapture.

Class 9: One bloom, division 6, white perianth (5). 1. R Scamp: Trena (Best Bloom in show). 2. D du Plessis: Trena. 3. R Nicholl: Trena.

Class 10: One stem, any other division (8). 1. R Scamp: S113. 2. C Skelmersdale: *N. intermedius*. 3. J Blanchard: 80/1B.

Class 11: One cultivar bred and raised by the exhibitor. (12). 1. R Scamp: S694. 2. R Nicholl: Congress × Achduart. 3. J Parkinson: 89-8.

Class 12: 3 miniature cultivars, one stem of each, bred and raised by the exhibitor (1). 1. J Blanchard: *N. atlanticus* X *N. asturiensis*, *N. asturiensis* X *N. cyclamineus*, Shillingstone.

Class 13: One miniature cultivar bred and raised by the exhibitor (6). 1. J Blanchard: 93/39. 2. Mrs E Bullivant: Cyclamineus cross. 3. J Blanchard: 63/2B.

Class 14: A species, or variety of a species of miniature narcissus, one stem. (8). 1. J Blanchard: *N. aureus* (Best miniature). 2. C Skelmersdale: *N. willkommii*. 3. R Wiseman: *N. tazetta gradicertinus*.

Class 15: One miniature cultivar, one stem. (8). 1. J Blanchard: Crevette. 2. C Skelmersdale: Sabrosa. 3. J Parkinson: Tête à Tête.

Class 16: An intermediate cultivar from divisions 1-4, one stem. (4). 1. D du Plessis: Sylph. 2. R Scamp: Radjel. 3. C Skelmersdale: Fairy Circle.

J. WALKERS BULBS
The specialist division of Taylors Bulbs

Gold Medal Daffodils for Showing & Growing

OVER 400 VARIETIES OLD AND NEW TO CHOOSE FROM

Large SAE for catalogue to:
Washway House Farm, Holbeach, Spalding, Lincs PE12 7PP

RHS Daffodil Show

Len Olive

Listening to the comments before the show on 13-14 April the usual seasonal problems which all exhibitors have to encounter, such as flowers being too early, too many cold days and nights, too much rain at the wrong time, were as evident this year as in any other. With all these problems, I was a little apprehensive as to what I could expect to see.

Nowadays, it seems most exhibitors have the skills and ingenuity with methods of weather protection to be able to keep their blooms in good condition whatever the weather throws at them. This certainly turned out to be the case this year. Consequently the show was one of the best in recent years, both in terms of superb quality blooms and the 943 stems staged in 416 entries.

Trade stands

In the past trade stands were a main feature of the London shows. Sadly in recent years they have become much less in evidence, almost to the point of complete absence. This year we were privileged to see two magnificent trade displays along the side wall. John and Rosemary Pearson of Hofflands Daffodils' staged a long high-tiered stand which contained no less than 90 impeccably staged vases of exhibition varieties, many of their own raisings. The overall effect was very pleasing and justly deserved the Gold Medal it was awarded.

The second trade stand (see back cover) was a combined effort of four growers, each having an equal amount of space. This exhibit, again a high-tiered one, was put on by R A Scamp Daffodils, Broadleigh Gardens, J Walker's Bulbs and Brian Duncan Daffodils. The combined effort was very pleasing and well received by all. Let us hope that this may be the way forward and that others will follow. This stand was also awarded a Gold Medal. As would be expected, each of the four had different types of flowers on show.

R A Scamp had a good mixture of ten division 4 cultivars plus many blooms from division 5 to 9. Broadleigh Gardens, the miniature specialists, put up a superb display of reliable species and hybrid miniatures. Vases of 'Paula Cottell', 'Rikki', N. *canaliculatus* and N. *intermedius* were outstanding. In my opinion this display deserved an award on its own. J Walker's Bulbs staged a very colourful stand made up of the more popular dual purpose exhibition and garden cultivars. Many of these cultivars are still able to hold their own on the show bench, with 'Whitbourne', 'Eminent' and 'Bithynia' being his best. Brian Duncan included several first generation split-corona daffodils on his stand. Three that really caught my eye were the seedling 11aW-P 'Movie Star' × 'Last Chance' along with 'Diversity' and 'Trigonometry'. All looked very promising.

Seedling Classes

The premier trophy, the Engleheart Challenge Cup for twelve cultivars raised by the exhibitor attracted four entries. Everyone likes to see new varieties and this year it was very pleasing to see 20 seedlings under number staged in this class alone. I have confined my comments to the seedlings.

The winner was Clive Postles who staged a well balanced exhibit which included nine seedlings. Most of Clive's seedlings were worthy of mention, but two really stood out. 1-29-86. 2Y-YYO was Best Bloom division 2 and Best Bloom in show (see Fig. 1). 1-43-87 was a very good 3Y-Y. 'Nice Day' from this collection was awarded Best Bloom division 3.

Brian Duncan was second. He went more for the tried and trusted of his introductions using only three seedlings; 2077 2Y-R, 1977 1Y-Y and 1742 2W-P, the latter two looking very promising.

67

In his third placed exhibit John Pearson included two unregistered seedlings 99-32/U106, an outstanding 2W-R and 99-22/U21.

Noel Burr was placed fourth. Amongst his six unregistered seedlings, 2-34-93 1W-P and 8-11-83 3Y-Y were outstanding. Credit must go to Noel who grows less than 1,500 bulbs but remarkably keeps turning out outstanding seedlings each year.

The Six seedling class was won by John Blanchard. Flowers which stood out were 'Ringwood' and seedling 89/40A 2Y-YYO. In his second placed entry Eddie Jarman showed six seedlings under number; among which 673 was a very nice 2W-W.

Third place went to Sir Frank Harrison, whose very nice set had no surprises as all were named cultivars.

In fourth place Ron Scamp staged a very credible set which included four numbered seedlings, all of division three flowers. S914 3Y-Y looked very good.

Amateur Collection Classes

The Bowles Challenge Cup is perhaps the most demanding of all. This class calls for fifteen cultivars from not fewer than four divisions, three stems of each, so it was very pleasing to see three exhibitors. Eddie Jarman was the winner (see Fig. 24) showing outstanding vases of 'Dorchester', 'Badbury Rings' and 'Dateline'. Second place went to Richard Gillings, whose best were 'Hartlebury' and 'Holme Fen'. John Ennis took the remaining place. Credit must go to John as he had cut his flowers more than a week before the event and sadly a few were beginning to show the tell-tale signs of age.

The Richardson Trophy for twelve cultivars representing each of divisions 1 to 4, one stem of each, attracted five entries. This class always seems to produce top quality flowers and this year was no exception. Derek Bircumshaw took the honours with an immaculate twelve which included outstanding blooms of 'Fireblade', 'Nice Day' and 'Moon Shadow'. Mr & Mrs D Marshall from Colchester in Essex took the second spot including good blooms of 'Midnight' and 'June Lake'. Third place went to Roger Braithwaite, his best being 'June Lake' and 'Dunley Hall'. The remaining places were taken by John Goddard and David Matthews.

Open Single Bloom Classes

Particularly noteworthy flowers in the open single bloom classes were Brian Duncan's 'Goldfinger', 1685 11W-YP ('Movie Star' × 'Last Chance') and 1798 11W-P ('Lady Ann' × 'Last Chance'); Eddie Jarman's 'Dorchester' which was Best Bloom division 4; David Matthews' 'Silent Valley' which was Best Bloom division 1; Paul Payne's 'Purbeck' and 'Moonshadow' and Clive Postles' 7-65-83 1Y-Y and 5-48-89 4W-Y.

Division 5 to 9 classes were well supported with the awards being well distributed. John Blanchard produced a magnificent 'Mission Bells' to win its class against very stiff competition and to win the Best Bloom division 5 to 9 award. John also excelled in the miniature classes and again was awarded the Best Miniature for 'Fairy Chimes'.

The award for most points in the single bloom classes went to Brian Duncan with Mrs Pam Cox from Maidstone runner-up.

Other Classes

Regrettably there were no entries staged for the Guy Wilson Memorial Vase. Brian Duncan won the class for six cultivars raised outside Europe from four other competitors.

The Horticultural Society's award was won for the first time by Ilkeston & District Chrysanthemum Society, with Wokley Horticultural Society close behind in second place. Norfolk & Norwich Horticultural Society, last year's winner in this class, failed to include a division 1 flower in their exhibit and duly received the dreaded N.A.S.

The Novice Section seems to get better every year. Many of the blooms would not have been out of place in the open section. Best Bloom in this section was awarded to D Griffin for an excellent 'Evesham' and he also won the Blanchard Prize for most points.

Show Results

Peter Wilkins

The number in brackets denotes the number of entries in each class.

Open Classes for new cultivars

Class 101: The Engleheart Challenge Cup, 12 cultivars, bred and raised by the exhibitor, one stem of each. (4). 1. F C Postles: 7-65-83, 1-148-90, 1-43-87, 2-148-90, 1-88-93, 1-36-95, 1-21-86, 1-29-6 (Best Bloom - Best Division 2), Samsara, Nice Day (Best Division 3), 1-56-90, Royale China. 2. B S Duncan: Arleston, Doctor Hugh, Bouzouki, Queen's Guard, Assertion, 2077, Cisticola, Ethos, Gold Ingot, June Lake, 1977, 1742. 3. A J Pearson: 99-32-U106, Monks Wood, Barnwell Mill, Altun Ha, Lighthouse Reef, Half Moon Caye, Celestial Fire, Lavender Mist, Guy Wilson, 99-22-U21, Sweet Sue, Clouded Yellow. 4. N Burr: Sharnden, Southease, Finchcocks, 2.34.93, 1.36.93, 1.11.85, 2.60.93, 1.59.89, Motts Mill, Fire Ashes, 8.11.83, Cinder Hill.

Class 102: Silver Simmonds Medal, six cultivars, bred and raised by the exhibitor, one stem of each. (4). 1. J Blanchard: 74/7A, Powerstock, Ringwood, 89/40A, 89/17A, 80/34F. 2. E Jarman: 341, 671, 651, 634, 410, 635. 3. Sir Frank Harrison: April Armour, Ballymorran, Barley Wine, Crown Imperial, Baltic Shore, Mexico City.

Class 103: Simmonds Medal, three cultivars, bred and raised by the exhibitor, one stem of each. (3). 1. J Gibson: 1-10-88, 2-6-89, 5-16-92. 2. J Parkinson: 92-4-7, 92-4-9, 92-4-1. 3. D du Plessis: 83/57/3, 83/72/7, 88/3.

Class 104: Simmonds Medal, three cultivars from divisions 5 to 9, bred and raised by the exhibitor, one stem of each. (2). 1. B S Duncan: Reggae, Kaydee, Georgie Girl. 2. R A Scamp: S581, S768, S920.

Class 105: Three cultivars - division 11, bred and raised by the exhibitor, one stem of each. (1). 1. B S Duncan: 1685, Diversity, 1798.

Class 106: One intermediate cultivar from divisions 1-4, bred and raised by the exhibitor, one stem (4). 1. B S Duncan: Signorina. 2. B S Duncan: Urchin. 3. R A Scamp: S910.

Class 107: Three cultivars, not in commerce, three stems of each. (1). 1. B S Duncan: 1387, 1749, 1791.

Class 108: Three miniature cultivars, bred and raised by the exhibitor, one stem of each. No entries.

Class 109: One miniature cultivar, bred and raised by the exhibitor, one stem. (1). 1. J W Blanchard: 77/14A.

Open classes for collections

Class 110: The Guy Wilson Memorial Vase, six cultivars of white daffodils representing any or all of divisions 1 to 3, three stems of each. No entries.

Class 111: Three cultivars representing one or more of divisions 1 to 3, three stems of each. (2). 1. A J Pearson: Sweet Sue, Goff's Kaye, Celestial Fire. 2. B S Duncan: Silver Surf, Ethos, Cisticola.

Class 112: Three cultivars, division 4, three stems of each. (3). 1. B S Duncan: Dorchester, Dunkery, Dunadry Inn. 2. D du Plessis: Inara, Smokey Bear, Gay Kybo. 3. R A Scamp: Gay Kybo, Bere Ferrers, Jamaica Inn

Class 113: Three cultivars representing one or more of divisions 5 to 9, three stems of each. (3). 1. R A Scamp: Life, Bunting, S554. 2. B S Duncan: Georgie Girl, Elfin Gold, Dimple. 3. D du Plessis: Killearnan, Stratosphere, Sextant.

Class 114: Three cultivars, division 11, three stems of each. (1). 1. B S Duncan: 1723, Diversity, 1819.

Class 115: Three cultivars from any or all of divisions 1 to 3, with pink colouring in the corona, three stems of each. (2). 1. B S Duncan: Pulsar, Chanson, Ice Dancer. 2. No award

Overseas collections

Class 116: Six cultivars, from any division or divisions raised outside Europe, one stem of each. (5). 1. B S Duncan: Cryptic, Berceuse, Colourful, Miss Primm, Pop's Legacy, Conestoga. 2. J Goddard: Oakland, Marque, Conestoga, Demand, Immaculate, Bandit. 3. M J Brook: Star Trek, Nonchalant, Baldock, Ivory Gull, Cool Crystal, Conestoga.

Open to Horticultural Societies

Class 117: Silver Simmonds Medal, 12 cultivars representing each of divisions 1 to 4, one stem of each. Open only to any Horticultural Society, other than a specialist Daffodil Society or Group. (3). 1. Ilkeston & District Chrysanthemum Society: Dr Hugh, Goldhanger, Evesham, Ffitches Folly, Altun Ha, Honeybourne, Liverpool Festival, Pol Voulin, Glen Alladale, Fireblade, Dorchester, Goldfinger. 2. Wokley Horticultural Society: Miss Primm, Serena Lodge, Ethos, Thoresby, Royal China, Chobe River, Loch Alsh, Gold Bond, Twicer, Satin Doll, Solar Tan, Moon Shadow. 3. No award.

Open classes for miniatures and intermediates

Class 118: Miniature narcisi, three species, three stems of each. (1). 1. J W Blanchard: N.panizzianus, N.jonquilla henriquesii, N.nevadensis.

Class 119: Miniature narcissi, three hybrids, three stems of each. (2). 1. T Braithwaite: Segovia, Hawera, Xit. 2. R A Scamp: Xit, Sun Disc, Segovia.

Class 120: Miniature narcissi, one species or variety of a species, three stems. (1). 1. R A Scamp: *N.jonquilla*.
Class 121: Miniature narcissi, one hybrid, three stems. (5). 1. J W.Blanchard: Fairy Chimes (Best miniature). 2. R J Wiseman: Hawera. 3. R A Scamp: Segovia.
Class 122: One intermediate cultivar from divisions 1 to 4, three stems. (1). 1. B S Duncan: Urchin.

Single bloom or stem

Class 123: 1Y-Y (19). 1. B S Duncan: Goldfinger. 2. F C Postles: 7-65-83. 3. L Olive: Goldfinger.
Class 124: 1Y-W or Y-WWY (8). 1. B S Duncan: Trumpet Warrior. 2. Mr & Mrs D Marshall: Lighthouse Reef. 3. A J Pearson: Lighthouse Reef.
Class 125: 1Y-any other colour. (8). 1. D G Matthews: Filoli. 2. R Braithwaite: Corbiere. 3. B S Duncan: 2079.
Class 126: 1W- with yellow in the corona. (6). 1. B S Duncan: Queen's Guard. 2. N Watson: Drumlin. 3. M Bird: Asante.
Class 127: 1W-W (14). 1. D G Matthews: Silent Valley (Best division 1). 2. R Chantry: White Star. 3. J Wickes: Panache.
Class 128: 1W-any other colour. (5). 1. B S Duncan: Chanson. 2. L Olive: Pink Silk. 3. G Ridley: Pink Silk.
Class 129: 2Y-Y (14). 1. G Ridley: Bulbarrow. 2. D G Matthews: Gold Convention. 3. B S Duncan: Arleston.
Class 130: 2Y- with red and/or orange in the cup predominant. (20). 1. B S Duncan: Cease Fire. 2. A J Pearson: Doctor Jazz. 3. R J Wiseman: Liverpool Festival.
Class 131: 2Y- with red and/or orange in the cup but not predominant. (7). 1. P Payne: Fireblade. 2. M Baxter: Fireblade. 3. B S Duncan: 2065.
Class 132: 2Y-W or Y-WWY (12). 1. G & V Ellam: Altun Ha. 2. A J Pearson: Altun Ha. 3. J Wickes: Altun Ha. 4. P Payne: Altun Ha.
Class 133: 2Y-P or any other Y- not eligible for classes 129 to 132. (4). 1. B S Duncan: 2080. 2. R A Scamp: Kings Pipe. 3. J W Blanchard: Chemeketa.
Class 134: 2O-O or R (6). 1. G Ridley: Cosmic Dance. 2. B S Duncan: Limbo. 3. S Holden : Bailey.
Class 135: 2W- with red and/or orange in the cup predominant. (9). 1. L Mace: Royale Marine. 2. A J Pearson: 99-40-U104. 3. D G Matthews: Young Blood.
Class 136: 2W- with red and/or orange in the cup but not predominant. (8). 1. J W Blanchard: Ringleader. 2. J.Wickes: Ringleader. 3. M.Brook: Ringleader.
Class 137: 2W-Y or W-WWY (12). 1. J.W.Blanchard: 86/22A. 2. F C Postles: Severn Valley. 3. G Ridley: Fiona MacKillop.
Class 138: 2W- with pink in the cup predominant. (19). 1. F C Postles: 10-19-89. 2. A.J.Pearson: Fine Romance. 3. N Burr: 1-14-87.
Class 139: 2W- with pink in the cup but not predominant. (18). 1. F C Postles: Royale China. 2. R A Chantry: June Lake. 3. B S Duncan: June Lake.
Class 140: 2W-W (20). 1. D G Matthews: Silk Cut. 2. Mr & Mrs D.Marshall: Inverpolly. 3. R Braithwaite: Hanbury.
Class 141: 3Y-Y (10). 1. B S Duncan: Ferndown. 2. E Jarman: Riseden. 3. L Olive: Citronita. 4. N Burr: 8.11.83.
Class 142: 3Y- with red and/or orange in the cup predominant. (13). 1. P Payne: Dateline. 2. B S Duncan : Jake. 3. R Braithwaite: Achduart.
Class 143: 3Y- with red and/or orange in the cup but not predominant. (17). 1. G & V Ellam: Badbury Rings. 2. F C Postles: 2-56-90. 3. P Hurren: Badbury Rings. 4. Mrs P R Cox: Badbury Rings.
Class 144: 3O-O or R (6). 1. D G Matthews: Sabine Hay. 2. B S Duncan: War Dance. 3. J W Blanchard: Sabine Hay.
Class 145: 3W- with red and/or orange in the cup predominant. (14). 1. F Verge: Cairntoul. 2. D Bircumshaw: Dr. Hugh. 3. B S Duncan: Hawangi. 4. P Payne: Rockall.
Class 146: 3W- with red and/or orange in the cup but not predominant. (17). 1. P Payne: Purbeck. 2. F Verge: Shropshire Lass. 3. A J Pearson: Sweet Sue. 4. D .G Matthews: Purbeck.
Class 147: 3W-Y or W-WWY (16). 1. P Payne: Moon Shadow. 2. J M Parkinson: Moon Shadow. 3. F C Postles: Moon Shadow.
Class 148: 3W-W (15). 1. Mrs P Cox: Verona. 2. B S Duncan: Silver Crystal. 3. J Goddard: Cool Crystal.
Class 149: 3 other than those eligible for classes 141 to 148. (3). 1. B S Duncan: Eyrie. 2. No award. 3. Mrs P Cox: Cupid's Eye.
Class 150: 4Y-Y (8). 1. R A Scamp: Marjorie Treveal. 2. S Alexander: Marjorie Treveal. 3. Mrs P Cox: Marjorie Treveal.
Class 151: 4Y-O or R (14). 1. F C Postles: Crowndale. 2. E Jarman: 257. 3. F Verge: Crowndale.
Class 152: 4W-W or Y (12). 1. F C Postles: 5-48-89. 2. L Olive: Unique. 3. R A Scamp: Unique.
Class 153: 4W-P (5). 1. E Jarman: Dorchester (Best division 4, Reserve Best Bloom). 2. B S Duncan: Dorchester. 3. R A Scamp: Pink Paradise.

Class 154: 4W-O or R (5). 1. J M Parkinson: Gay Kybo. 2. P Payne: Gay Kybo. 3. R A Scamp: Gay Kybo.

Class 155: One Stem Div 4 other than those eligible for classes 150-154. (2). 1. B S Duncan: Double Day. 2. J W Blanchard: Double Day.

Class 156: 5Y- with white or colour in the cup. (1). 1. B S Duncan: 93/33.

Class 157: 5W- with colour in the cup. (2). 1. Mrs P Cox: Tuesday's Child. 2. B S Duncan: Chorus Line.

Class 158: 5W-W (10). 1. J W Blanchard: Mission Bells (Best species hybrid). 2. Mrs P Cox: Ice Wings. 3. L Olive: Ice Wings. 4. B S Duncan: Ice Wings.

Class 159: 6Y-Y or Y-W (7). 1. M Bird : Rapture. 2. Mrs M Bird: Rapture. 3. Mrs T Braithwaite: The Alliance.

Class 160: 6Y-O or R (1). 1. No award.

Class 161: 6W-Y (1). 1. No award. 2. B S Duncan: Phalarope.

Class 162: 6W-O , P or R (6). 1. G Ridley: Georgie Girl. 2. A J Pearson: Katrina Rea. 3. B S Duncan: Lilac Charm.

Class 163: 6W-W (7). 1. B S Duncan: Sheer Joy. 2. J Goddard: Sheer Joy. 3. G Ridley : Sextant.

Class 164: 7Y-Y (6). 1. Mrs P Cox: Sweetness. 2. D du Plessis: Stratosphere. 3. No award.

Class 165: 7Y or O with red and/or orange and/or pink in the cup. (7). 1. Mrs P Cox: Bunting. 2. D du Plessis: Bunting. 3. G &V Ellam: Stratosphere.

Class 166: 7Y-W (5). 1. J W Blanchard: Oryx. 2. B S Duncan: Intrigue. 3. Mrs P Cox: Intrigue.

Class 167: 7W- with white or colour in the cup. (6). 1. E Jarman: Ladies Choice. 2. G & V Ellam: Sweet Blanch. 3. D du Plessis: Eland. 4. J W Blanchard: Bell Song.

Class 168: 8Y- with colour in the cup. (5). 1. G Ridley: Highfield Beauty. 2. Mrs P Cox: Falconet. 3. B S Duncan: Seedling.

Class 169: 8W- with white or colour in the cup. (6). 1. Mrs P Cox: Geranium. 2. G & V Ellam: Avalanche. 3. P Hurren: Silver Chimes.

Class 170: Division 9 (10). 1. J Goddard: Killearnan. 2. B S Duncan: Kamau. 3. R Wiseman: Killearnan.

Class 171: Division 11 Yellow Perianth. (3). 1. B S Duncan: 1940. 2. Mrs P Cox: Gironde. 3. R A Scamp: Tripartite.

Class 172: Division 11 White Perianth. (1). 1. B S Duncan: Diversity.

Class 173: A hybrid intermediate narcissus from divisions 1 to 4. (5). 1. B S Duncan: Brooke Ager. 2. G Ridley. Urchin. 3. P Hurren: Bantam

Class 174: Miniature narcissus, a species or variety of a species. (4). 1. J W Blanchard: N. panizzianus. 2. R J Wiseman: N. bulbocodium
3. R A Scamp: N. jonquilla

Class 175: Miniature narcissus, a hybrid. (6). 1. J W Blanchard: 77/14A. 2. R J Wiseman: Clare. 3. No award.

Class 176: Division 12. (1). 1. R A Scamp: S350.

Amateur Section

Class 178: The Bowles Challenge Cup, 15 cultivars, representing not fewer than four divisions, three stems of each. (3). 1. E Jarman: Silverwood, Badbury Rings, Dorchester, Garden News, 673, Gold Ingot, Masaka Sun, State Express, Pure Joy, Rosegold, Soprano, Triple Joy, Young Blood, Dateline, 705. 2. R Gillings: Hartlebury, Verwood, Gull, Twicer, Holme Fen, Miss Primm, Honeybourne, Goldfinger, Royal Marine, Hambledon, Severn Valley, Crackington, Rainbow, Barnesgold, Ravenhill. 3. J S Ennis: Gold Bond, Rushmore, Dunkery, Hambledon, Silent Valley, Moon Valley, Front Royale, June Lake, Jambo, Goldfinger, Ahwahnee, Purbeck, Dunadry Inn, Bossa Nova, Royale Princess.

Class 179: The Richardson Trophy, 12 cultivars, representing each of divisions 1 to 4, one stem of each. (5). 1. D Bircumshaw: Aircastle, Altun Ha, Inverpolly, Ombersley, Goldfinger, Pol Crocan, Fireblade, Moonshadow, Nice Day, Chateau Impney, Gay Kybo, Cape Cornwall. 2. Mr & Mrs D.Marshall: Gin & Lime, Loch Alsh, Arleston, April Love, Evesham, Finchcocks, Pol Crocan, Altun Ha, Greetham, June Lake, Midnight, Gay Kybo. 3. R Braithwaite: Evesham, Cape Cornwall, Silent Valley, Pol Crocan, Lighthouse Reef, June Lake, Colourful, Goldhanger, Gay Kybo, Greetham, Purbeck. 4. J H Goddard: June Lake, Happy Fellow, Dunley Hall, Grand Prospect, Demand, Dorchester, Golden Jewel, Loch Alsh, Dailmanach, Gold Bond, High Society, Ethos. HC. D G Matthews: Sweet Sue, Goldfinger, Silent Valley, Gold Convention, Paradigam, Ashmore, Verwood, Dr. Hugh, Southease, Fire Hills, Young Blood, Coromandel.

Class 180: Six cultivars, representing not fewer than three divisions, one stem of each. (7). 1. F Verge: Young Blood, Barnesgold, June Lake, Cool Crystal, Dateline, Colleygate. 2. J Gibson: Loch Alsh, Corbiere, Gold Convention, Pol Crocan, Purbeck, Liverpool Festival. 3. J M Parkinson: Cool Crystal, Altun Ha, Dr. Hugh, Evesham, Samsara, Gay Kybo. 4. M J Brook: Eastern Promise, Dateline, Altun Ha, China Doll, Serena Beach, Jackadee.

Class 181: Three cultivars, division 1, three blooms of each. No entries

Class 182: *Three cultivars, division 2Y- white or coloured cup, three blooms of each.* (1). 1. R.Gillings: Twicer, Surrey, Loch Carron
Class 183: *Three cultivars, division 2W- white or coloured cup, three blooms of each.* No entries
Class 184: *Three cultivars, division 3, three blooms of each.* (1). 1. M J Brook: Cool Crystal, Syracuse, Silverwood
Class 185: *Three cultivars, division 4, three stems of each.* No entries
Class 186: *One cultivar, division 5, three stems.* (1). 1. R J Wiseman: Waxwing.
Class 187: *One cultivar, division 6, three blooms.* (3). 1. Mrs P Cox: Elfin Gold. 2. Mrs T Braithwaite: The Alliance. 3. R J Wiseman: Kaydee.
Class 188: *One cultivar, division 7, three stems.* (2). 1. Mrs P Cox: Pipit. 2. J Smith: Oryx.
Class 189: *One cultivar, division 8, three stems.* (3). 1. Mrs P Cox : Geranium. 2. P Hurren: Silver Chimes. 3. R J Wiseman: Silver Chimes.
Class 190: *One cultivar, division 9, three blooms.* (3). 1. R J Wiseman: Killearnan. 2. Mrs P Cox: Cantabile. 3. J Smith: Killearnan.
Class 191: *One cultivar, division 11, three blooms.* (2). 1. J Smith: Seedling. 2. Mrs P Cox: Gironde.
Class 192: *Six cultivars, one stem of each, registered in or before 1975.* (1). 1. E Green: Ringleader, Dailmanach, Euphony, Rubh Mor, Ashmore, Achduart.
Class 193: *Six cultivars, one stem of each, registered in or before 1965.* (1). 1. E Green: Lysander, Panache, Unique, Rainbow, Merlin, Verona.
Class 194: *Three cultivars, three stems of each, registered in or before 1955.* No entries.
Class 195: *Three cultivars, bred and raised by the exhibitor, one stem of each.* (3). 1. J M Parkinson: 93-12, 93-2-9, 92-8-9. 2. J Gibson: 3-3-90, 1-2-91, 3-6-89. 3. L Olive: Strines O.P., White Star × Canisp, Kingscourt × Gold Convention.
Class 196: *One cultivar, bred and raised by the exhibitor, one stem.* (3). 1. F Verge: Fiona MacKillop. 2. J Goddard: Inverpolly O.P. 3. J Goddard: Inverpolly O.P.

Novice classes
Class 197: *Six cultivars, representing not fewer than three divisions, one stem of each.* (3). 1. R Springthorpe: Liverpool Festival, Evesham, Silent Valley, Aircastle, Purbeck, White Star. 2. S Alexander: Bere Ferrers, Cool Crystal, Rainbow, Marjorie Treveal, Irish Light, Merlin. 3. D Griffin: Altun Ha, Thoresby, Evesham (Best Bloom Novice Classes), Ethos, Crowndale, Nether Barr.
Class 198: *Three cultivars, division 1, one bloom of each.* (1). 1. D Griffin: Golden Vale, Hadlow Down, Ethos.
Class 199: *Three cultivars, division 2, one bloom of each.* (3). 1. D Griffin: Hambledon, Bailey, Tyrian Rose. 2. R Springthorpe: S33, Misty Glen, Zapollo. 3. S Alexander: Rainbow, Ringleader, Irish Light
Class 200: *Three cultivars, division 3, one bloom of each.* (3). 1. R Springthorpe: Dunley Hall, Aircastle, Evesham. 2. D Griffin: Ridgecrest, Evesham, Orange Walk. 3. S Alexander: Advocat, Merlin, Cool Crystal

Novice single bloom or stem
Class 201: *1Y- with colour in the corona.* (2). 1. S Alexander: St Budock. 2. D Griffin. Cheetah.
Class 202: *1Y-W or Y-WWY* No entries.
Class 203: *1W- with colour in the corona.* (1). 1. D Griffin: Elmbridge
Class 204: *1W-W* (1). 1. D Griffin: Sherpa.
Class 205: *2Y-Y* (2). 1. D Griffin: Gold Bond. 2. No award.
Class 206: *2Y- with red and/or orange in the cup.* (2). 1. D Griffin: Liverpool Festival. 2. S Alexander: Gettysburg.
Class 207: *2Y-W or Y-WWY* (2). 1. B Stewart: Altun Ha. 2. D Griffin: Altun Ha.
Class 208: *2W- with red and/or pink and/or orange in the cup.* (4). 1. B Stewart: Lakeland Fair. 2. S Alexander: Rainbow. 3. D Griffin: Neon Light.
Class 209: *2W-Y or W-WWY* (1). 1. S Alexander: Westholme.
Class 210: *2W-W* (2). 1. B Stewart: White Tea. 2. D Griffin: Chinchilla.
Class 211: *3Y- with red and/or pink and/or orange in the cup.* (1). 1. D Griffin: Chickerell.
Class 212: *3W- with red and/or pink and/or orange in the cup.* (4). 1. B Stewart: Sugar & Spice. 2. S Alexander: Merlin. 3. D Griffin: Evesham.
Class 213: *3W-W* (1). 1. S Alexander: Cool Crystal.
Class 214: *Division 4* (4). 1. R Chantry. Gay Kybo. 2. S Alexander: Marjorie Treveal. 3. D Griffin: Crowndale. 4. C Drury: Gay Kybo.
Class 215: *Division 5* (1). 1. S Alexander: Arish Mell.
Class 216: *Division 6* (1). 1. D Griffin: Elfin Gold.
Class 217: *Division 7* (1). 1. S Alexander: Stratosphere.
Class 218: *Division 8* (1). 1. S Alexander: Silver Chimes.
Class 219: *Division 9* No entries.
Class 220: *Division 11* No entries.

RHS Late Daffodil Competition

Reg Nicholl

I have the pleasure of commenting on the last daffodil show at the RHS this century, or even millennium come to that. The extremely early season meant that the Late Competition held on 27-28 April suffered from a scarcity of entries with only 157 stems staged in 68 entries from about a dozen competitors. For the same reason, most flowers lacked real quality, although there were a few excellent flowers to be seen.

Trade Stand

Trade or Display stands are rare at this Competition so it was pleasing to see Martin Harwood, holder of the National Collections of daffodils, stage 36 vases covering ten types of cultivar, from pre-1887 'White Lady' 3W-Y to present day ones, for which he was awarded a Bronze Medal.

Collection Classes

Brian Duncan was the only entrant in the John Lea Trophy for twelve seedlings raised by the exhibitor, one stem of each. His winning entry included some excellent flowers amongst which was a superb 'Goldfinger' 1Y-Y which was Best Bloom division 1, the doubles 'Serena Beach' 4W-Y and 'Dorchester' 4W-P and an extremely fine 3Y-R seedling D1589 as smooth in petal as one would wish.

The other seedling classes, five in all, received scant support. However in the single seedling class was Eddie Jarman's 357, another example of which was Best Bloom in show (see below). Eddie also took second place with a neat division 3 bloom 719, just beating Jim Davidson of Banff, Scotland who showed 86/48 3W-YYO which had a flat white perianth and a nice orange rim.

The Devonshire Trophy for twelve cultivars from at least three divisions, one stem of each, drew an admirable four entries and enabled Brian Duncan to capture his second major trophy. 'Suntrap' 2Y-YYR, 'Naivasha' 2W-P and 'Hawangi' 3W-R were his outstanding flowers. Runner-up was David Matthews who staged excellent blooms of 'Savoir Faire' 2W-GWP, 'Silver Crystal' 3W-GWW and a neat 3Y-O seedling 1511 which I understand because of a canine connection is now named 'Little Polly'.

The amateur's class for a collection of six cultivars from at least three divisions, one stem of each resulted in a narrow victory for Richard McCaw over Len Olive. He showed superb flowers of 'Naivasha' and the infrequently seen Reg Wootton raising 'Fairy Island' 3W-GOO. Len staged particularly fine blooms of 'Burning Bush' 3Y-R and 'Notre Dame' 2Y-GYP. Third was Jim Davidson who included a lovely flower of the rather under-rated 'Dateline' 3Y-O in his half dozen.

Single Blooms

The trumpet daffodils were generally found wanting as might be expected given the early season and there were few outstanding flowers in this group. The pick were the two 'Mulroy Bay' 1Y-Y shown by Brian Duncan and Richard McCaw respectively in Class 315. The large cupped types were perhaps the best segment in the event. Best Bloom in Show and Best Bloom division 2 was awarded to Eddie Jarman's seedling 357, which won Class 327 which calls for one bloom division 2 with a white perianth and red or orange in the cup predominant. 357 featured a neat white perianth. However, it was the depth of red colour in most of the corona which was most arresting. It was subsequently named 'Garden Party'

2W-WRR. As noted on page 50 'Garden Party' was later awarded the Ralph B White Memorial Medal. It is pictured on the front cover.

Len Olive produced an imposing 'Liverpool Festival' 2Y-O to win its predominant colour class. Richard Gillings also had a grand flower of 'Hambledon' 2YYW-Y. The small cupped classes were reasonably well supported and one very interesting flower was shown by Brian Duncan, an all yellow seedling of immaculate form 92-12 which looks distinctly promising. His 'Triple Crown' 3Y-GYR also took first prize in its class in which Richard McCaw and Len Mace with the same cultivar created a clean sweep. Brian Duncan continued his successes with a superb double, 'Dorchester' 4W-P which won its class. However, it was overshadowed by David Matthews' superlative 'Gay Kybo' 4W-O which was Best Bloom division 4.

Support for the remaining divisions was patchy but Richard McCaw showed a consummate all yellow cyclamineus seedling 1257 and capped a fine all-round show performance by staging a peerless 'Cantabile' 9W-GYR to capture the Best Stem from Divisions 5 - 9 and 11, which was also selected as the Reserve Best Bloom.

Other Classes

Using the previously mentioned poeticus Richard McCaw also won the newly created class for seven cultivars, Jim Davidson being in second place. Although it contained only two entries, the class created a pleasing spectacle and was well worth introducing.

However, one aspect of the show was most disappointing, there being no entries in the Novice Section.

SHOW RESULTS

Peter Wilkins

The number in brackets denotes the number of entries staged in the class.

Class 301: Silver-Gilt Simmonds Medal, twelve cultivars, bred and raised by the exhibitor, one stem of each. (1). 1. B S Duncan: Serena Beach, Goldfinger (Best Bloom division 1), Dr. Hugh, D 1589, Garden News, D 1648, Suntrap, Savoire Faire, Dorchester, Triple Crown, Naivasha, Arizona Sunset.

Class 302: Silver Simmonds Medal, six cultivars, bred and raised by the exhibitor, one stem of each. No entries

Class 303: Silver Simmonds Medal, three cultivars, bred and raised by the exhibitor, and representing at least two of divisions 5 to 9, one stem of each. No entries

Class 304: One unregistered cultivar, bred and raised by the exhibitor, one stem. (3). 1. E Jarman: 357. 2. E Jarman: 719. 3. J Davidson: 86/48

Class 305: One miniature cultivar, bred and raised by the exhibitor, one stem. No entries

Class 306: One intermediate cultivar, bred and raised by the exhibitor, one stem. (1). 1. No award. 2. J Davidson: 94/48.

Class 307: Miniature narcissus, three species, three stems of each. No entries

Class 308: Miniature narcissus, three hybrids, three stems of each. No entries

Class 309: Miniature narcissus, one species or variety of a species, three stems. No entries

Class 310: Miniature narcissus, one cultivar, three stems. (3). 1. R McCaw: Sun Disc. 2. L Mace: Sun Disc. 3. J Davidson: Hawera.

Class 311: One intermediate narcissus from divisions 1 to 4, three stems. No entries

Class 312: The Devonshire Trophy, 12 cultivars, representing not fewer than three divisions, one stem of each. (4). 1. B S Duncan: Goldfinger, Hawangi, Garden News, Savoire Faire, June Lake, Sun Trap, Naivasha, Sperrin Gold, Badbury Rings, Ridgecrest, Little Karoo, Singin Pub. 2. D Matthews: Dailmanach, Ahwahnee, June Lake, Sperrin Gold, Fireblade, Savoire Faire, D1511, Gay Kybo, Silver Crystal, State Express, Nether Barr, Unknown. 3. R F Gillings: State Express, Holme Fen, Royal China, Ethos, Ice Dancer, Barnesgold, June Lake, Twicer, Solar Tan (Best Bloom Division 3), Wychavon, Furnace Creek, Jocelyn Thayer. 4. J Davidson: Mentor, Cairngorm, China Doll, Altun Ha, Dateline, Royal Princess, Goldfinger, Silkwood, Nether Barr, Ferndown, Vernal Prince, Bossa Nova.

Class 312a: One or more cultivars from division 9, seven stems. (2). 1. R McCaw: Cantabile. 2. G W Goddard: Cantabile.

Class 313: Silver Simmonds Medal, 12 cultivars, representing not fewer than three divisions, one stem of

each. Open to any horticultural Society other than a specialist daffodil society or group. No entries
Class 314: Six cultivars, representing three or more divisions, one stem of each (Daffodil Society Southern Championship, third leg). No entries
Class 315: 1Y-Y (5). 1. R McCaw: Mulroy Bay. 2. B S Duncan: Mulroy Bay. 3. D G Matthews: Sperrin Gold.
Class 316: 1Y-W, or Y-WWY No entries
Class 317: 1Y-any other colour. (1). 1. D G Matthews: York Minster.
Class 318: 1W-W (4). 1. R McCaw: White Star. 2. L Olive: April Love. 3. No award.
Class 319: 1W- with yellow in the corona. (2). 1. No award. 2. B S Duncan: Queen's Guard. 3. G & V Ellam: Asante.
Class 320: 1W-any other colour. (1). No award.
Class 321: 2Y-Y (5). 1. L Mace: Golden Sheen. 2. R Gillings: Miss Primm. 3. No award
Class 322: 2Y- with red and/or orange in the cup predominant. (4). 1. L Olive: Liverpool Festival. 2. R McCaw: Patabundy. 3. R Gillings: Red Spartan.
Class 323: 2Y- with red and/or orange in the cup but not predominant. (3). 1. D G Matthews: Fireblade. 2. No award. 3. R Gillings: Twicer.
Class 324: 2Y-W or WWY (2). 1. J Davidson: Altun Ha. 2. B S Duncan: Altun Ha.
Class 325: 2Y-P or any other Y- not eligible for classes 321 - 324. (1). 1. R Gillings: Hambledon.
Class 326: 2O-O or R (2). 1. B S Duncan: Limbo. 2. D G Matthews: Dawn Run.
Class 327: 2W- with red and/or orange in the cup predominant. (4). 1. E Jarman: Garden Party (Best Bloom division 2). 2. J Davidson: Nether Barr. 3. R Gillings: Nether Barr.
Class 328: 2W- with red and/or orange in the cup but not predominant. (1). No award
Class 329: 2W-Y or W-WWY (2). 1. L Mace: Holme Fen. 2. No award
Class 330: 2W- with pink in the cup predominant. (8). 1. J.Davidson: Mentor. 2. L.Olive: Dailmanach. 3. E.Jarman: 93-41-4.
Class 331: 2W- with pink in the cup but not predominant. (8). 1. E Jarman: Notre Dame. 2. R McCaw: Movie Star. 3. R Gillings: June Lake.
Class 332: 2W-W (7). 1. R Gillings: Hanbury. 2. D G Matthews: Callander. 3. L Olive: Misty Glen.
Class 333: 3Y-Y (3). 1. B S Duncan: 92/12. 2. D G Matthews: Lalique. 3. J Davidson: Ferndown.
Class 334: 3Y- with red and/or orange colouring in the cup predominant. (6). 1. R F Gillings: Solar Tan. 2. R McCaw: Arizona Sunset. 3. B S Duncan: Garden News.
Class 335: 3Y- with red and/or orange colouring in the cup but not predominant (5). 1. B S Duncan: Triple Crown. 2. R McCaw: Triple Crown. 3. L Mace: Triple Crown.
Class 336: 3O-O or R. No entries
Class 337: 3W- with red and/or orange in the cup predominant. (4). 1. J Davidson: Glendarroch. 2. E Jarman: Crimson Chalice. 3. D G Matthews: Crimson Chalice.
Class 338: 3W- with red and/or orange in the cup but not predominant. (6). 1. E Jarman: Carole Lombard. 2. J McCaw: Royale Princess. 3. L Olive: Carol Lombard.
Class 339: 3W-Y (8). 1. R McCaw: Dunley Hall. 2. L Olive: Halley's Comet. 3. R Gillings: Halley's Comet.
Class 340: 3W-W (6). 1. J Davidson: Cool Crystal. 2. G Riley: Warmington. 3. E Jarman: Silverwood.
Class 341: Other than those eligible for classes 333-340. No entries
Class 342: 4Y-Y No entries
Class 343: 4Y-O or R (3). 1. D G Matthews: Golden Bear. 2. L.Mace: Crowndale. 3. R McCaw: Moralee.
Class 344: 4W-W or Y (4). 1. E Jarman: Serena Lodge. 2. D G Matthews: Unique. 3. B S Duncan: Serena Beach.
Class 345: 4W-P (5). 1. B S Duncan: Dorchester. 2. E Jarman: Pink Pageant. 3. L Olive: Postles Seedling.
Class 346: 4W-O or R (3). 1. D G Matthews: Gay Kybo (Best Bloom division 4). 2. J Davidson: Gay Kybo. 3. E Jarman: Cavendish.
Class 347: other than those eligible for classes 342 - 346. (1). 1. K Blundell: Sir Winston Churchill.
Class 348: 5Y- with colour in the cup. (2). 1. G & V Ellam: Hawera. 2. D G Matthews: Hawera.
Class 349: 5W- with colour in the cup. (2). 1. L Olive: Tuesday's Child. 2. K Blundell: Tuesday's Child.
Class 350: 5W-W (2). 1. K Blundell: Mission Bells. 2. G & V Ellam: Rippling Waters.
Class 351: 6Y-Y or 6Y-W (3). 1. R McCaw: 1257. 2. B S Duncan: Elfin Gold. 3. J Davidson: Rapture.
Class 352: 6Y- with red and/or orange in the cup. No entries
Class 353: 6W-Y (2). 1. G & V Ellam: Jack Snipe. 2. J Davidson: 93/1.
Class 354: 6W- O, P or R (3). 1. B S Duncan: Elizabeth Ann. 2. R McCaw: Lilac Charm. 3. K Blundell: Foundling
Class 355: 6W-W (3). 1. L Olive: Sheer Joy. 2. G Ridley: Sextant. 3. G & V Ellam: Jenny.
Class 356: 7Y-Y (3). 1. B S Duncan: Stratosphere. 2.

J Davidson: Stratosphere. 3. G & V Ellam: Quail.
Class 357: 7Y or O, with red and/or orange colouring in the cup. (3). 1. L Mace: Stratosphere. 2. K Blundell: Indian Maid. 3. No award
Class 358: 7Y-W (2). 1. K Blundell: Oryx. 2. G & V Ellam: Oryx.
Class 359: 7W- with white or colour in the cup. (1). 1. G & V Ellam: Sweet Blanche.
Class 360: 8Y- with white or colour in the cup. (1). 1. G & V Ellam: Unknown.
Class 361: 8W- with white or colour in the cup. (2). 1. G & V Ellam: Silver Chimes. 2. K Blundell: Geranium.
Class 362: Division 9 (8). 1. R McCaw: Cantabile (Best Specie Hybrid, Reserve Best Bloom). 2. E Jarman: 329. 3. J Davidson: Ireland's Eye.
Class 363: Division 11 with Yellow perianth. No entries
Class 364: Division 11 with White perianth. No entries
Class 365: A miniature species, one stem. No entries
Class 366: A miniature hybrid, one stem. (3). 1. J Davidson: Hawera. 2. R McCaw: Bebop. 3. L Mace: Sun Disc.
Class 367: An intermediate narcissus from divisions 1 - 4. No entries

Amateur classes

Class 368: Seven stems of one or more cultivars from all or any of divisions 1, 2 or 3. (2). 1. R McCaw: Savoire Faire, Cupid's Eye, Naivasha, Amboseli, Arizona Sunset, Triple Crown, Samsara. 2. J Davidson: Unnamed.
Class 369: Six cultivars, representing not fewer than three divisions, three stems of each. No entries
Class 370: Six cultivars, representing not fewer than three divisions, one stem of each. (3). 1. R McCaw: Moralee, Birchwood, Naivasha, Samsara, Triple Crown, Fairy Island. 2. L Olive: April Love, Evesham, Altun Ha, Burning Bush, Fireblade, Notre Dame. 3. J Davidson: Altun Ha, Purbeck, Silkwood, Dateline, Gay Kybo, Royal Princess.
Class 371: Three cultivars, representing one or more of divisions 5 to 8, one stem of each. No entries
Class 372: Three cultivars, division 9, one stem of each. No entries
Class 373: Three cultivars, division 11, one stem of each. No entries

Novice classes

In all the following classes there were no entries
Class 374: One bloom 1Y- with colouring in the cup.
Class 375: One bloom 1Y-W or Y-WWY
Class 376: One bloom 1W- with colouring in the cup.
Class 377: One bloom 1W-W.
Class 378: One bloom 2Y-Y
Class 379: One bloom 2Y-R/O
Class 380: One bloom 2Y-W or Y-WWY
Class 381: One bloom 2W- with red and/or orange and/or pink in the cup.
Class 382: One bloom 2W-Y
Class 383: One bloom 2W-W
Class 384: One bloom 3Y- with colouring in the cup.
Class 385: One bloom 3W- with colouring in the cup.
Class 386: One bloom 3W-W
Class 387: One stem division 4.
Class 388: One stem division 5.
Class 389: One bloom division 6.
Class 390: One stem division 7.
Class 391: One stem division 8.
Class 392: One stem division 9.
Class 393: One stem division 11.

RHS Tulip Competition

James L Akers

The Tulip Competition held at Westminster on 27 to 28 April, was once more disappointing because there were only three exhibitors.

Miss M Charlwood is a regular exhibitor here and once again was able to make two entries in most of the classes. Miss Charlwood's best entry was probably 'Canova' with which she won the class for three blooms of fringed cultivars. Her other first prize was gained with 'Angélique' in the class for double tulips.

The happiest exhibitor however was Mrs A Ware, better known in the worlds of tulips, journalism and broadcasting as Anna Pavord. Having spent the last six years in writing her wonderful book *The Tulip* which is reviewed on page 54, she entered her very first tulip competition. In total she won four first, two second and one third prizes but it was to win class 1 for nine blooms of one or more cultivar with 'Prinses Irene' (see Fig. 3) which gave her the most joy. For the first time the winner of this class was awarded The Walter Blom Trophy. Anna was presented with the trophy by Walter's son Ron Blom at the meeting of the Daffodil and Tulip Committee which followed the judging.

The other competitor was Wendy Akers who made the long journey from Yorkshire with little success.

At next year's show a simpler schedule, where many classes are by colour rather than classification, will be used. So please buy some bulbs and bring some flowers along to the show!

Show Results

The number in brackets denotes the number of entries staged in the class.

Class 1: One vase of nine blooms, one or more cultivars The Walter Blom Trophy (5).1. Mrs A Ware: Prinses Irene. 2. Miss M Charlwood: Appeldoorn's Elite × 3, West Point × 3, Black Swan × 2, Red Wing. 3. Mrs W M Akers: Pink Impression.

Class 2: Single early cultivars, one vase of three blooms (1) 1. Mrs A Ware: Purple Prince.

Class 3: Double early or double late cultivars, one vase of three blooms (2). .1. Miss M Charlwood: Angélique. 2. Miss M Charlwood: Mount Tacoma. 3. No award.

Class 4: Triumph or mid-season cultivars, one vase of three blooms (8). 1. Mrs A Ware: Meissner Porzellan. 2. Mrs A Ware: Prinses Irene. 3. Mrs A Ware: Couleur Cardinal.

Class 5: Single late cultivars, one vase of three blooms (3).1. Miss M Charlwood: Black Swan. 2. Mrs A Ware: Magier.

Class 6: Lily flowered cultivars, one vase of three blooms (2). 1. No award. 2. Miss M Charlwood: Maytime.

Class 7: Fringed cultivars, one vase of three blooms (2). 1. Miss M Charlwood: Canova. 2. Miss M Charlwood: Red Wing.

Class 8: Viridiflora cultivars, one vase of three blooms (2). 1. No award. 2. No Award. 3. Miss M Charlwood: Spring Green

Class 9: Parrot cultivars, one vase of three blooms (1).1. No award. 2. No award. 3. Mrs W M Akers: Weber's Parrot.

Class 10: Kaufmanniana, greigii, or fosteriana cultivars, one vase of three blooms (1).1. No award. 2. Mrs W M Akers: Czar Peter

Class 11: Darwin hybrid cultivars, one vase of three blooms (3). 1. Mrs A Ware: Unknown. 2. Miss M Charlwood: Appeldoorn's Elite. 3. Mrs W M Akers: Pink Impression

Class 12: Any species, one pot or pan of five bulbs in bloom (1) 1. No award. 2. Mrs W M Akers: *T. clusiana* var *Chrysantha*.

STEVE HOLDEN DAFFODILS

New supplier of quality exhibition daffodil bulbs
FROM THE WORLD'S LEADING
HYBRIDISERS

Top quality bulbs for all exhibitors; beginners
through to the very experienced.

After many personal successes on the show bench,
Steve Holden is now growing and supplying
bulbs to other exhibitors.

This year's catalogue has new introductions

Write or phone for your free copy:

Steve Holden Daffodils
Sunny Corner, Copse Lane
Walberton, Arundel, West Sussex
BN18 0QH

Telephone or Fax: 01243 542070

Other Shows

The Daffodil Society Show

Jim Pearce

Such is the capricious nature of an English spring, that inevitably there are lean years and years of abundance. Unfortunately this was not a year of plenty and so the Daffodil show on 17-18 April suffered the same fate as all the other major events. A particularly early season combined with above average temperatures undoubtedly was responsible for the shortfall. Even so, despite some notable omissions most of the staging was well filled.

It is our good fortune to be associated with Solihull Horticultural Society in the presentation of the event. Their side of the business helping in no small manner in giving added impetus and interest particularly for the general public. To this must be added the several local branches of national bodies that regularly give them their support

From a high of five trade displays a few years ago Ron Scamp alone kept the flag flying with his Herculean sized group well representing the divisions. All were gathered from the open from what is reckoned the warmest and so earliest part of the mainland. Lynne and Jan Dalton staged a potted version of their outstanding memorabilia collection that provoked much interest at the Centenary Show

The Bourne Cup

Unlike its London counterpart, the Bourne Cup, the major trophy for seedlings raised by the exhibitor attracted but one entry - not an unfamiliar sight over the years. All the more credit then to Clive Postles for his effort in presenting a well balanced set with the customary hallmark of top line staging, though perhaps slightly less spectacular than in former years. Keen eyes soon homed in on 149-91 2Y-R, which had an airing for Best Bloom, no mean feat in itself though to some extent expected from this class.

Open Collection Classes

Next in line of seniority among the cups is the Cartwright Challenge Cup calling for twelve cultivars in commerce. Derek Bircumshaw who has won for several years had to be content with second place with our more recent exhibitor Roger Braithwaite leading the field with a very well staged and pristine set. Derek was not too disappointed his immaculate, and I use that word advisedly, 'Inverpolly' gained him the newly instituted Jim Pearce award for the show's Premier Bloom.

James Barrington, a past treasurer of the society who as the then Chair of Solihull Society was instrumental in forming the initial liaison between the societies enjoyed a particular interest with, dare I say it, the lower divisions. His passing presented the opportunity for an award to his memory. He would have been very flattered to note that this class calling for six cultivars from those divisions was so well supported. There were five entrants, Alan Robinson triumphed and featured a very fine 'Petrel' boasting six florets.

Few classes have escalated in support more than that calling for six cultivars with pink in the corona. This year some five entrants filled the staging led by Steve Holden. His 'Lakeland Fair' may well have enjoyed greater fame but for a minor irregularity in one petal.

There were three contestants in The White Daffodil Trophy for six white trumpets. Chris Yates' entry which won included a notable 'Quiet Waters' if rather square in the cup.

The Leamington Challenge Cup which requires six cultivars with orange or red in the cup from any division had five contestants with Ray Hayward leading the field.

Alan Robinson unfortunately had a rather hollow victory as the only entrant in the Williams Challenge Cup which is generally reckoned an easy class to enter - six yellows any division.

Both the Arkwright Challenge Cup and Dr Lower Cup classes failed to excite an entry with the latter possibly the least contested class over the years. Making up for lost ground The Ernie Darlow Memorial Award, instituted in his honour for his many years in the chair and his particular love of whites, attracted six contestants. Roger Braithwaite triumphed and yet another 'Inverpolly' shone forth. The American Daffodil Society Red, White and Blue ribbon went to Ian Tyler and fittingly President George Tarry collected the first award for three Australasian cultivars.

Amateur Trophy Classes

These were mostly well supported with a general tenor of quality. Alan Robinson mustered a very creditable exhibit to take the de Navarro Challenge Cup and his 'Gold Convention' looked particularly impressive. Unfortunately he was the sole entrant though nevertheless worthy of the trophy.

Six seedlings raised by the exhibitor enabled P Mills to take home the Knight Cup. His 3W-Y, 91/42A attracted most attention with a noticeably frilled expanded corona.

The Post & Mail, Webb, Sankey and GKN trophies each requiring three cultivars in a single vase were well supported in the price restriction classes with seven entrants in the Sankey, red and/or orange being required in the coronas. M Henson emerged the victor. Roger Braithwaite triumphed in this sections, premier trophy class the Norfolk requiring twelve threes. His immaculately staged group contained fine examples of 'Tutankhamun', 'Rainbow' and 'Ravenhill'.

The Peter Lower Challenge Trophy goes to the winner of the Societies Class. It was good to see a new name in the lead, that of the Wrekin Horticultural Society. Old stagers Walsall came second with Bristol District in third place. Peter would have felt well satisfied.

The Woodward cup for the Best amateur bloom was easily won by A Greenwood for a superb 'Unique'.

Clive Postles collected the F E Board Trophy for the Best unregistered seedling, a 3Y-YOO, an improved 'Badbury Rings', which was also Best Bloom division 3. The judges had little difficulty in selecting John Pearson's fine vase of three 'Clouded Yellow' for the Bikini Vase award which also earned him the Society's Silvered Medal. This is another of John's subtle colour breaks of outstanding form.

The high profile F E Board Memorial Award was deservedly won by Alan Smith. 'Serena Beach', 'Goldfinger' and 'Nether Barr' formed his superbly staged entry. 'Goldfinger' looked particularly good but for a slight irregularity in its coronas which spoilt it's chances for Best vase of three.

Single Bloom Classes

In the single bloom classes Clive Postles had a notable success with a 3Y-Y seedling which had a smooth buttercup yellow cup with slightly paler perianth. D Hockley stole the limelight with his 'Silent Valley' as the Premier Bloom in this section. John Pearson's newly registered 'Sergeant's Caye' 1YYW-WWY showing its strong 'Daydream' and 'Gin and Lime' influence caused a fair degree of interest. A vintage 'Strines' put Derek Bircumshaw in the lead of division 2 yellows. Another friend from former years 'Tutankhamun' placed Ian Yeardley to the fore, a fine example which arrived just in time!

Once again 'Dailmanach' proved it's worth among the well supported pinks class. 'Caribbean Snow' 2YYW-W continued the winning streak of lime coloured flowers synonymous with John Pearson to win the Best Bloom division 2. 'Dorchester' was again preeminent in its class and a beautiful tailored 'Rapture' was Best Bloom division 5-9.

In a very difficult season many blooms showed the stress of time. There was a distinct sameness with a clutch of good flowers but really outstanding ones were noticeably absent.

Tulips at Alpine Garden Society Shows

Alan Edwards

Bulb enthusiasts who prefer to drool over species rather than hybrids nowadays have their interests well catered for at the various national shows of the Alpine Garden Society. In recognition of the fact that our winters are becoming progressively more benign with a consequent significant advance in flowering dates, the Society now stages two non-competitive shows in early February, firstly at Carleon followed a week later by another at Loughborough. As one would expect these two events produce enchanting displays of early *Narcissus* with a supporting cast of Crocus, *Galanthus* and a few liliaceous items such as Colchicum and Scilla. Subsequent, but competitive shows during March at Harlow, again at Loughborough and Morecambe always feature large entries in the classes for *Narcissus* species. Devotees of the genus *Tulipa* will usually find a few species on show at Harlow, even in early March and such was the case this year when *T. T. kurdika, humilis violacea* and *neustruevae* appeared on the benches.

For those afflicted seriously with the modern equivalent of tulipomania the AGS Kent Show held at Rainham in the third week of March can always be relied upon to provide relief. This year, among the ranks of quiet-toned *Narcissus* and *Fritillaria*, the classes for *Tulipa* species shone out like beacons. Among the most fiery were two fine pans of *T. schrenkii*, a taxa often lumped under *T. armena* by some or considered to be synonymous with *T. suaveolens* by others, but nevertheless a very fine species for the show bench. *T. schrenkii* is a native of the steppe lands of southern Russia where it occurs in various colours from white through yellow to red. It is the later which is normally seen in cultivation and was on display here. Even more brilliant was a pan of seed-raised *T. stapfii*, an infrequently seen but very typical member of the dramatic oculis-solis group from North and West Iran. This exhibit contained several huge blood-red flowers with yellow-edged black centres which were effectively displayed against a foil of glaucous foliage. Also raised from seed and rivalling the aforementioned for brilliance was *T. julia*, a fairly short-stemmed species with large scarlet, black-eyed flowers which, in this example, lacked a yellow zone - a feature which created a striking effect. This fine tulip was found in the Zap Gorge in Hakkari Province in South East Turkey, but its range extends onwards through Transcaucasia into Iran. The bulbs in this exhibit first flowered in 1990 from a sowing made in 1986. This illustrates how relatively quickly quite large flowered species will mature from seed and also attest to the longevity of the bulbs when well cared for in a well ventilated bulb frame and given that all-important warm, dry summer dormancy.

Two smaller species, namely *T. cretica* and *T. neustruevae* were also represented, the former from the sun-scorched mountain ridges of Greece's largest island, may be had in either green or pink-backed forms, but both have white interiors which create a pleasing contrast when partially open. The species is stoloniferous which can create a problem for the tidy minded in a well ordered bulb frame. I have an enduring recollection of finding a large colony in full bloom among the shattered grey rocks, cresting the top of a ridge in southern Crete. The dainty pink and white blooms made an indelible impression when viewed against the backdrop of the azure sea below. *T. neustruevae* is increasingly seen at the shows these days. It will perform well both in the open and in a pan. The flowers are golden yellow with an external median green stripe and some purplish suffusion. It is a native of Central Asia and may well grow in company with the similar but better know *T. dasystemon*.

At the A G S main Spring Show at Vincent Square on 13 to 14 April there were surprisingly few tulips still about. Just one glorious pan of *T. aucheriana* appeared in the six pan (bulbous) competition for the Frank Waley Cup. This tulip from N Iran is often downgraded as a mere variant of *T. humilis* but the material on display was, to my mind, most distinguished with many starry well presented flowers of an enchanting cyclamen pink.

Wakefield and North of England Tulip Society 164th Annual Show

Richard Smales

In a year badly affected by tulip fire in Yorkshire entries suffered and the overall standard was down. On the brighter side, the occasion could almost have been renamed Ladies' Day as between them they almost monopolised the trophies.

The Dutch tulip classes were badly affected by tulip fire. The Peter Emmett Trophy for the best Dutch exhibit was won by Mrs Sylvia Madden with six 'Black Parrot' tulips.

The classes for broken English Florists' Tulips were also fire affected but Mrs Sarah Wainwright rescued sufficient to take four trophies. She had probably picked them early because the fire struck just before the show. Her success in the Needham Memorial Cup for twelve dissimilar rectified English Tulips made her only the third person to win it since her grandfather, Jim Akers, many years ago. The entry contained Best Feather in Show with 'Sir Joseph Paxton'. She also won the Stages Cup and the Cochrane of Cults Vase, again with 'Sir Joseph Paxton', and the Jim Akers Memorial Goblet for most points in the Open Classes.

The breeder classes were a walk-over for Mrs Beryl Royles of North Wales. Her twelve different breeders which won the Norman Eyre Memorial Goblet contained the best breeder and winner of the Albert Tear Memorial Trophy for the overall Premier Bloom. It was a bizarre breeder R59. She naturally took the G S Hunter Memorial Cup for six breeders and the Silver Plate for three breeders along with the seedling cup. I say "naturally" because unfortunately the only person who could have given her any kind of competition was John Wainwright who was devastated by fire.

The contribution that Peter and Beryl Royles are making to the English Florists' tulip cannot be over emphasised. Their displays are unprecedented. The colours of the new breeders cover a range of mahogany, magenta and burgundy, all with their clear yellow or white base and their open flat-topped, half tennis ball shape. To the enthusiast, these are the most beautiful tulips ever produced.

Peter and Beryl have fallen in love with the solid coloured breeder tulips, but in so doing they have created a paradox.

They no longer grow "broken" or virus affected bulbs. They wish they had never introduced the breaking virus into their growing environment. As soon as an emerging flower shows signs of "breaking" they remove the bulb and destroy it so that the virus is not passed on. Peter deeply regrets the 300 seedlings he has sacrificed to this end. In turn we shall never know whether good "flames" and "feathers" have been lost forever.

I know of other tulip growers who wish they had never introduced broken English tulips into their gardens. The virus remains in the ground. It induces garish patterns in Dutch tulips. Broken English tulips are a specialist flower nurtured by florists for the purpose of competition. They may look nice in the border, but a stand of breeders is in my opinion, a better proposition.

In retrospect then, I believe the Royles are taking the correct course. The variety and quality they have created in the English breeder tulip is too precious to jeopardise. If in the fullness of time they have stock to distribute and it subsequently breaks attractively, then so be it, but in the meantime, Peter and Beryl, keep producing those breeders. The tragedy on the day was that tulip fire robbed us of John Wainwright's seedling breeders.

The fourth lady to whom the day was memorable was Mrs Barbara Pickering, a relative newcomer to English Florists' tulips. She won the Brooke Silver Challenge Cup for most points in the Novice Classes and the Stan Knowles Cup for most points and Best Bloom in the Extra Open Classes. Interestingly, Barbara grows in the middle of the "fire zone" but saw none. She has recently moved house and her new garden had not grown tulips before. This confirms the adage that the fungus is in the ground and when temperature and moisture are favourable fire will appear overnight.

I will give the final word to the breeder tulips. The Novice and Extra Open Classes include classes for breeders as does the Gina Roozen Cup for three breeders, all were well supported. Practically every breeder shown in these classes had come from the Hortus Bulborum in Holland by one route or another. The occasional releases they have made over several years have kept breeder tulips alive at this level in the society. Without Dutch supplies there would have been no exhibits. We are very grateful to the Hortus Bulborum for maintaining virus-free stocks and wish them to know there are always ready homes for excess bulbs.

Daffodils and Tulips at Harrogate

Richard Smales

Exhibiting daffodils in the latter half of April must provide the most compelling evidence for global warming. I hope I am wrong, otherwise, in the year 2000 when Harrogate is a week later, there will be no daffodils at all.

It follows that each of the 63 exhibitors is to be commended, but on the first day there were dead flowers among the 1020 shown, and apart from the blue rosette champion blooms the standard was down on a normal year.

North of England Championship
Colin Gilman was a good winner of the North of England Championship for the second year running but I am sure he would agree they were well below his usual standard. Colin struggled for yellows and included two reversed bicolours - the ever dependable 'Altun Ha' and 'Lighthouse Reef' adjudged Champion 1Y-W and Reserve Grand Champion. Like last year he used 'Unique' as his double. It was clean and fresh but not really championship material.

In second place Dennis Marshall of Colchester staged good but tired blooms of which the ubiquitous 'Altun Ha' was best, R Chantry's third placed exhibit had the Grand Champion 'Gay Kybo'; a really memorable flower; full, round and fresh. He also had a lovely 'Fragrant Rose' with a pronounced rose flush to the perianth.

Other Collection Classes
Dennis Marshall succeeded in Class 2 for six from four divisions with 'Dunley Hall' his best flower, though overall the set lacked colour. There were no entries in Class 3 for six trumpets.

Class 4 is for six all yellow cultivars and the first three placings were alive but not good. Unplaced were Roger Braithwaite's six which contained five blooms - 'Ballyrobert', 'Ethos', 'Goldfinger', 'Goldhanger' and 'Midas Touch', better than any other five in the class. Unfortunately he completed his six with a washed out 'Citronita' which the judges refused to acknowledge. It is many years now since the late and sadly missed Geoff Bell did exactly the same, in the same class. The judges refused to have any tack with it then. The reaction of the two exhibitors in question was similarly vociferous.

Roger managed to bounce back with his six whites, 'Hanbury' being the best and his 'Inverpolly' very smooth. He also took the class for six with red or orange in the cup, but it was an impoverished class of only three entries and many flowers, particularly his 'Twicer' were approaching death. Roger's wife Terry took the award for six blooms from divisions 5 to 9 and her 'Arish Mell' I thought particularly good.

The Daffodil Society Northern Group's Open Class for three cultivars from three divisions, three stems of each deservedly went to Dennis Marshall for three excellent vases of 'Altun Ha', 'Badbury Rings' and 'Goldfinger'. The set had size and colour but no white perianths. Christine Yeardley's second placed exhibit had a good vase of 'Misty Glen'. First and second in the vase for one cultivar from division 1 were both 'Goldfinger' for Jeff Stuart and Ron Crabtree respectively. The winners particularly had good size along with the usual substance of this cultivar. 'Goldfinger' is establishing itself as the 1Y-Y every exhibitor must have because it is so consistent. In the class for three from division 2 Paul Payne triumphed with 'Neon Light' one of which was Champion division 2 W-R. One of Colin Gilman's second placed set of 'Coromandel' was Champion division 2Y-Y. The three from division 3 and division 4 went to Paul also with vases of 'Moon Shadow' and 'Gay Kybo'. I commented last year on how well Paul grows (and whitens) 'Moon Shadow' and his entry in the single blooms was the Champion 3W-Y.

Classes 13 to 16 for vases of three blooms compete for the Jack Morley Memorial Trophy and it went to L Tomlinson of Claveley, Cheshire for his vase of three pinks. His 'Satin Doll' was very smooth and his Mitsch seedling KK17/2 showed particularly good colour and was Champion Seedling.

The three miniatures went to 'Sun Disc' staged by J Parkinson of Bolton and the Champion Miniature was a 'Sun Disc' also, in the unplaced exhibit of Cliff Bilbrough. D McDonald of Whickham won the three species with *N. bulbocodium* subsp. *bulbocodium* var. *conspicuus* and he also took the single bloom with *N. odorus* 'Campernelli plenus'.

Single Bloom Classes

The single bloom classes were notable for the number of blue rosette champion blooms they contained and were dominated by Paul Payne and Colin Gilman of Norwich and Jeff Stuart of Wombwell, Barnsley. Paul had 'Eastern Promise', 'Badbury Rings', 'Cool Crystal' and 'Moon Shadow'. Colin had Champion Blooms with 'Altun Ha' and 'Rockall' which is his speciality! Jeff had blue rosettes with 'White Star' and 'Dateline' and took the Jim Akers Seedling Class with a very smart 2Y-R 166/1 ('Shining Light' × 'Stanway').

Other Champion Bloom winners were Mrs S Parsons of Corby with 'Ice Wings; D McDonald with 'Rapture'; Mike Brook with 'Patois' and Jan Dalton with 'Tripartite'.

Price Limit Classes

The classes for bulbs costing no more than £1 were a triumph for Mick Henson of Heanor, Derbyshire. In the section open to exhibitors who have not won a major medal or trophy he took the Daffodil Society's Northern Group Crystal Trophy for six cultivars, the three cultivars all yellow; three all white and three with red or orange. His 'Ringleader', 'Misty Glen' and 'Ravenhill' were good flowers.

Trade Stands

In the Daffodil and Tulip Marquee R V Roger Ltd of Pickering staged three trade exhibits featuring daffodils, tulips and small bulbs. Their efforts are to be commended and they won two silver gilt and a bronze medal respectively. Pride of place in the trade exhibits went to Johnny Walkers who took the Premier Award for the Best Exhibit for the second time in three years. He exhibited 54 varieties totalling 1,500 blooms. Most had been in cold storage 2⁰c (35⁰F) but even then 17 varieties had been discarded at staging time. He was obviously light on yellows but one vase of 'Golden Aura' stood out. Probably its substance and shape help it to stand up to cold storage. Every exhibitor in the collection classes could have benefited by using one of these.

I began by commenting on the forward season. Johnny estimated he was five weeks ahead of a normal year, a pattern that had accrued over the last 15 years. He illustrated it with a 'Pheasant's Eye'. In some years he has to force it out for Chelsea Show. This year he cut it from the open ground for Harrogate, held some four weeks earlier than Chelsea.

Tulip Championship of Great Britain

And so to the inaugural Tulip Championship of Great Britain - three vases of nine tulips in three different varieties. There were ten entries in this class and similar support for the other classes. What a welcome blaze of colour they provided and most flowers stood up for the four days of the show. Let up hope that next year we can acquire a central stand to be viewed from both sides.

The clear champion was Derek Williams of Denton. The precision of his 27 blooms was reminiscent of his immaculate daffodil presentations. He showed 'Golden Oxford', 'Pink Impression' and 'Olympic Flame' (see Fig. 20). Many people have asked "what do you look for in exhibiting tulips?". It was all here. Each bloom was a full, round, two thirds of a goose egg. Broad overlapping petals of equal length and round when viewed from above. Does this sounds familiar? The stems were straight and strong so that the contents of each vase, and indeed vases, formed a plateau of equally spaced identical blooms. Add to this freshness and condition, the prerequisite when judging any floral exhibit and Derek set the standard for all the Championships we hope will follow.

Mr and Mrs King's second placed exhibit of 'Apeldoorn Elite', 'Oxford' and 'Golden Apeldoorn' were commendable as were exhibits throughout the show but the three vases for the first ever Tulip Championship of Great Britain will remain in the memory for a long time.

SOUTH EAST ENGLAND DAFFODIL GROUP

DAVID MATTHEWS

As usual the weather played its customary role in deciding which exhibitors would have their best flowers for our show on 11 April. This year flowers from divisions one and two suffered, and many of the entries for these which had been made the previous week failed to materialise on the day. Nevertheless 1300 vases were staged by 76 exhibitors making the 1999 show one to remember.

Seedlings

The Cinderella section of most shows is usually the seedlings, but this was certainly not true this year, for in here were to be found some of the most interesting amateur raisings seen for a long time. Peter Mills monopolised these classes winning all three with quality flowers that any professional would have been pleased to stage. One of Peter's best in the class for six seedlings was 91/42, a well rounded 3W-Y of great potential; and in the single seedling class his 94/61A was a 2W-W of pristine condition. John Gibson, Ron Allen and John Parkinson also showed very promising seedlings which would certainly have won red cards in any other year.

SEEDG Championship

Peter Mills' other major achievement was to win from eight exhibits the SEEDG Championship Trophy. His winning twelve included the Best Bloom in show - an excellent 'Dailmanach' shown alongside high quality examples of 'Gold Convention', 'Evesham', 'Achduart', 'Ulster Bank', 'Cool Crystal', 'Unique', 'Rockall', 'Cairntoul' and two of his own seedlings under number - 94/123 a 2Y-Y and 91/32 a clearly coloured 2O-R with a well defined cup. Second in the Championship was Frank Verge with Geoff Ridley third.

Other Classes

Mid Southern Daffodil Group made an instant impact on the Inter-Society Championship by winning the Jenny Trophy with good blooms of 'Loch Alsh', 'State Express', 'Altun Ha', 'Dailmanach', 'Cool Crystal' and 'Filoli'. Placed second was New Forest Chrysanthemum and Dahlia Society with Haywards Heath Horticultural Society third. There were nine entries of extremely high quality in this class, and a number of exhibitors must have given some of their best blooms to bolster their Society's entry.

A newcomer to the professional scene,

Steve Holden ably assisted by his wife Julia, set up their first trade stand, on which there were some fine flowers. Steve certainly made his presence felt on the show-benches winning the Best Exhibit in show with his Ted Osborne Memorial Class entry calling for two vases of five blooms. Steve's cultivars in this well-staged and balanced exhibit were 'June Lake', 'Val d'Incles', 'Moon Shadow', 'Soprano' and 'Verona', with 'Filoli', 'Goldfinger', 'Cape Cornwall', 'Magic Moment' and 'Jambo'.

The award for most points in the highly competitive Single Bloom section was also won by Steve, closely pursued by Mrs. Pam Cox. Among Steve's exhibits were good blooms of 'Cape Cornwall' registered as 2Y-R but with its cup colour non predominant in this instance, 'Coromandel', 'Ashmore' and 'June Lake'. Tom Handley's striking bloom of 'Welcome' a New Zealand variety fast gaining in popularity over here came first in the 2W-Y class from new arrival 'Corky's Song' and 'Buttermere Lake'. In the 2W-W class Frank Verge's own raising 'Silver Dream' came third, whilst Mike Baxter's 'Lakeland Fair' finished ahead in a very strong class of division 2 pinks. Frank however won in the 3Y-Rs with 'Dateline', a very under-estimated cultivar in my opinion, as very few cut flowers of this variety are not of show standard. Another New Zealand introduction shown by Tom Handley, 'Kiwi Solstice' finished second the 4Y-Rs splitting Alan Bowditch's 'Dunkery' in first place and Steve Holden's 'Crowndale' third.

Continuing his winning streak Steve Holden led the field in the Multi-Bloom section, taking the division 1 with 'Goldfinger' and division 3 with 'Cool Crystal'. Close on his heels however, were John Parkinson and Frank Verge.

Dominating in the six Cultivars Class was Len Olive showing a large smooth 'Lancelot', a beautiful 'Neahkahnie' which earned eight points out of a possible ten, 'Evesham', 'April Love', 'Lennymore' and 'Dailmanach'. Second and third here were Frank Verge and Steve Holden.

The class for three vases of three blooms was particularly strong, with seven good entries. The eventual winner was John Gibson with first class blooms of 'Gold Convention', 'Purbeck' and his own seedling 3-6-89. In the six doubles class the Jenny Medal winner was David Vivash, with John Semple and Norman Lincoln second and third. David's fine exhibit included a lovely 4W-P pink seedling raised by Clive Postles, 'Islander', 'Piraeus', 'Merrymeet', 'Serena Beach' and 'Crackington'. Henry Ovenden's 'Ice Wings', 'Pipit' and 'Shot Silk' deservedly triumphed over 16 other exhibits in the class for three cultivars from divisions 5 - 9.

It was heartening to see 13 competitors in the miniature classes where Peter Hurren had most points. Janine Doulton's superb pot of 'Solveig's Song' received the award for the Best Miniature Exhibit.

Some Outstanding Flowers

One of the talking points of the day was Geoff Ridley's five headed 'Ice Wings' which received the rosette for Reserve Champion Bloom. Jack Land's P1-43-74 originating from the single bloom class for 2W-O or R was judged the Best Unregistered Seedling, whilst Frank Verge picked up the rosette for Best Bloom division 3 with a large 'Cool Crystal', and John Goddard's well formed 'Dorchester' received the accolade of Best Bloom division 4. David Hockley collected the award for Best Bloom division 1 with 'Silent Valley', which was included in his winning entry in the Novices' Trophy.

Your scribe had entered a large number of classes, but unfortunately had to withdraw from 90 per cent of them as he fell ill during staging - still there is always next year...

Showing for the first time at Tonbridge were a number of new exhibitors whom we were delighted to welcome. We hope they will continue to support us into the 21st Century.

CITY OF BELFAST SHOW

WENDY AKERS

To be invited to join the judges at the daffodil show in Belfast held on 17 April 1999 was to fulfil my long held wish to visit Northern Ireland, albeit with some trepidation. The television and press coverage of Northern Ireland in England is so unremittingly negative it almost seemed as though we would be visiting a war zone. The reality, as we drove to Omagh through rolling fields with fine cattle and contented sheep, impressive villages and towns and a general air of utter normality had to be adjusted to. Of course, this is not to ignore the political stresses which continue as I write this in July, but none of this was visible to James and myself. Certainly, when we finally drove into Belfast and the Barnett Demesne and entered Malone House on the first morning of the Spring Flower Show we were aware that this show is a grand occasion. The entrance hall with its fine sweep of stairs had a glorious arrangement of tazettas and jonquils on a tall stand at the foot of the balustrade, framed with pale yellow broom, then rising upwards a swagging of ivy and more bunches of jonquils. We reached the daffodil show through several elegant rooms emerging into a large marquee. Here the group of judges were soon busily at work.

The Championship of Ireland, which pleasingly has the Richardson Cup as its trophy was won by Brian Duncan with a superb set of twelve flowers. Three days before Brian had been in London at the Daffodil Show knowing that gales and hail were battering his daffodils at home. These daffodils at the show had been rescued from the teeth of the gales and other exhibitors told hair raising stories of the terrible weather. However, all was serene on the show bench and Brian's twelve flowers had a good selection of his lovely all yellow daffodils; 'Goldfinger', 'Gold Ingot', 'Chobe River' and two seedlings, one with a very uncomplicated straight trumpet - 1957. It was interesting to compare the different shades of gold, 'Gold Ingot' really is well named with its cup of red-gold. Second in the Championship was Michael Ward of Dublin followed by Sandy McCabe of Ballymena. The quality of these blooms set the standard for the rest of the show, which was of the highest. Brian also had a wonderfully balanced set to win the Royal Mail Trophy for six Irish raised varieties and the W H Roese Bowl for five American raised varieties also went to Brian, again closely followed by Michael Ward and with Kate Reade in third place. I thought that Guy Wilson would have thoroughly approved of the vase of three 'Silver Crystal' which was part of Brian's winning entry for the Guy Wilson Trophy. In the next class, the Gilbert Andrews Trophy, Derrick Turbitt had a double whammy in his six. He had a truly excellent seedling, 9409, which became Best Seedling, a very fat yellow perianth and a cup of orange with an almost vermilion rim, plus a superb example of 'Regal Bliss' which became Best Bloom division 2. Ballydorn had two unusually coloured flowers in their six, 'Sandymount' and 'Golden Strand' both registered as 2Y-O which doesn't really do justice to the peachy, apricot, buff mixture. 'Sandymount' is 'Golden Amber' open pollinated and is also a Ballydorn raised flower, with a similar unusual colour mix. 'Golden Amber' was raised from 'Kilmorack' open pollinated; a Brodie of Brodie cultivar which had 'Fairy King' as one parent. Following a line of breeding to try to find out where a particular colour has come from can be a delightful exercise but I came to a stop with 'Gulliver' (P D Williams - Cornwall) because that parentage is not given but the pollen involved in 'Sandymount' has done some travelling; Ireland, Scotland, Lincoln and Cornwall. While on the subject of unusual colour Sandy McCabe won the class for the International Award which included a gorgeous vase of three 'Filoli' (John Lea) where the corona is described as "buff pink with yellow tones at base". At this point in the judging I became aware that a brass band had struck up on the lawn outside the marquee and realised that I had been so absorbed looking at gorgeous daffodils that I had hardly noticed it. I have pages of notes of these excellent flowers but a few chosen from many must suffice. In her entry for three vases of poeticus hybrids Kate Reade had three of her own raising; 'Braid Song', 2-19-78 and 4-9-81, the latter containing the winner of the W J Toal Award and Best Bloom from divisions 5 to 9. The chosen flower was most perfectly balanced and had that extra breadth in the perianth that just makes you gasp. Brian Duncan's 'Chanson', what can one say, a trumpet in lavender pink with a white rim as though it had had its face powdered. Nial Watson's 'Patabundy', a classic shape with a deep yellow back and the most solid orange cup, Richard McCaw's outstanding 'Young Blood', Derrick Turbitt's lovely smooth 'Pol Voulin', Robert Curry's 'Nonchalant', a really yellow division 3 and not one you have to use your imagination on. Brian Duncan's 'Terrapin' will challenge 'Badbury Rings' having a deeper yellow perianth and a very deep red defined rim. Ballydorn had a gorgeous 'Ballynichol' 3W-GYR which has a thick textured white perianth and a dark emerald green eye all focusing on a glowing red rim. I have a mental picture of Richard McCaw beaming as he held his 'Dorchester' to be photographed as the Best Bloom in Show. What a pleasure it was to see his son David win the Novice Championship of Ireland with a very good twelve, including a superb 'Misty Glen' and a young lady, Alice Watson who had the Best division 3 in the show with 'Port Noo' 3 W-Y. It was a great pleasure to spend time in the company of growers and exhibitors of such enthusiasm, Irish hospitality is legendary and certainly lived up to its reputation.

Awards to Daffodils, Snowdrops and Tulips

Certificate of Preliminary Commendation
Galanthus plicatus **'Augustus'** PC 6 March 1999, Joint Rock Garden Plant Committee, as a hardy flowering plant for exhibition. Exhibited by Dr C Grey-Wilson, The Black House, Fenstead End, near Hawkedon, Bury St. Edmunds, Suffolk IP29 4LH.

Galanthus plicatus **'Florence Baker'** PC 19 January 1999, Joint Rock Garden Plant Committee, as a hardy flowering plant for exhibition. Exhibited by Dr R Mackenzie, Barn Cottage, Shilton, Oxon OX18 4AB.

Narcissus × cazorlanus PC 10 April 1999, Joint Rock Garden Plant Committee, as a hardy flowering plant for exhibition. Exhibited by J I & M Young, 63 Craigton Road, Aberdeen AB15 7UL.

Tulipa kurdika PC 20 March 1999, Joint Rock Garden Plant Committee, as a hardy flowering plant for exhibition. Exhibited by Miss R A Cox, 29 St. Catherine's Road, Harrogate, North Yorkshire.

Award of Merit
Galanthus **'Bill Bishop'**. AM 16 February 1999, Joint Rock Garden Plant Committee, as a hardy flowering plant for exhibition. Exhibited by Dr R Mackenzie, Barn Cottage, Shilton, Oxon OX18 4AB

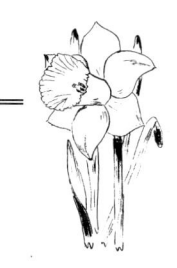

RA Scamp
Quality Daffodils

For a Colour Illustrated Catalogue of our Modern and Historical Daffodils.

Please send 3 first class stamps to:-
RA Scamp, 14 Roscarrick Close, Falmouth, Cornwall TR11 4PJ
Tel: 01326 317959

Carncairn Daffodils Ltd.
GOLD MEDAL DAFFODILS

For exhibition and for garden

send for free catalogue

Carncairn Grange Broughshane
Co. Antrim BT43 7HF

Telephone: 01266 861216
Fax: 01266 862842

Hofflands Daffodils

Suppliers of Quality Daffodil Bulbs to the World

Raisers of Many Top Prize-winning Varieties

R.H.S. Gold Medal 1995, 1998 & 1999

A.D.S. Trophy 1996 & 1997

Engleheart Cup 1995

Send for our free catalogue

JOHN & ROSEMARY PEARSON

Hofflands, Bakers Green, Little Totham,
Maldon, Essex. CM9 8LT. U. K.
E-Mail: sales@hoffdaff.kemc.co.uk
Telephone: (44) (0)1621 788678
Fax: (44) (0)1621 788445

DAFFODIL & TULIP COMMITTEE 1999

CHAIRMAN

Duncan, B S, Knowehead, 15 Ballynahatty Road, Omagh, Co Tyrone, N Ireland BT78 1PN

VICE-CHAIRMEN

Blanchard, J W, Old Rectory Garden, Shillingstone, Blandford, Dorset DT11 0SL
Pearce, D J, 1 Dorset Cottages, Birch Road, Copford, Colchester, Essex CO6 1DR

MEMBERS

Akers, J L, 70 Wrenthorpe Lane, Wrenthorpe, Wakefield, West Yorkshire WF2 0PT
Blom, R J M, Birwell Lodge, Shelton, Huntingdonshire PE18 0NR
Bradbury, M S, The Well House, 38 Powers Hall End, Witham, Essex CM8 1LS
Brandham, Dr P, Jodrell Laboratory, Royal Botanic Gardens, Kew, Richmond, Surrey TW9 3DS
Burr, N A, Rushers Cottage, Rushers Cross, Mayfield, East Sussex TN20 6PX
Dalton, J, 34 Conan Drive, Richmond, North Yorkshire DL10 4PQ
du Plessis, D, Upalong, Church Lane, Landulph, Saltash, Cornwall PL12 6NS
Hardy, G A, Hillhurst Farm, Hythe, Kent CT21 4HU (deceased February)
Jarman, E, Clover Meadows, Treraven Lane, Wadebridge, Cornwall PL27 7JZ
Lemmers, W, Freesiastraat 10, 2161 XM Lisse, The Netherlands
Matthews, D, 35 Hazeldown Close, River, Dover, Kent CT17 0NJ
Nicholl, R, 17 Orchard Avenue, Rainham, Essex RM13 9NY
Pearson, A J R, Hofflands, Bakers Green, Little Totham, Maldon, Essex CM9 8LT
Postles, F C, The Old Cottage, Purshull Green, Droitwich, Worcs WR9 0NL
Scamp, R, 14 Roscarrack Close, Falmouth, Cornwall TR11 4PJ
Skelmersdale, Lady, Barr House, Bishops Hull, Taunton, Somerset TA4 1AE
Tarry, G W, Cresta, Well Lane, Ness, Neston CH64 4AW
Walkers, J, Broadgate, Weston Hills, Spalding, Lincs PE12 6Q
Secretary Kington, Mrs S, RHS, 80 Vincent Square, London SW1P 2PE

NARCISSUS CLASSIFICATION ADVISORY COMMITTEE 1999

Chairman Blanchard, J W
Vice Chairman Pearce, D J
Bradbury, M S
Brickell, C D
Duncan, B S

Gripshover, Mrs M L
Lemmers, W
Nicholl, R
Secretary Kington, Mrs S
Ex officio Leslie, A C

The National Daffodil Society of New Zealand

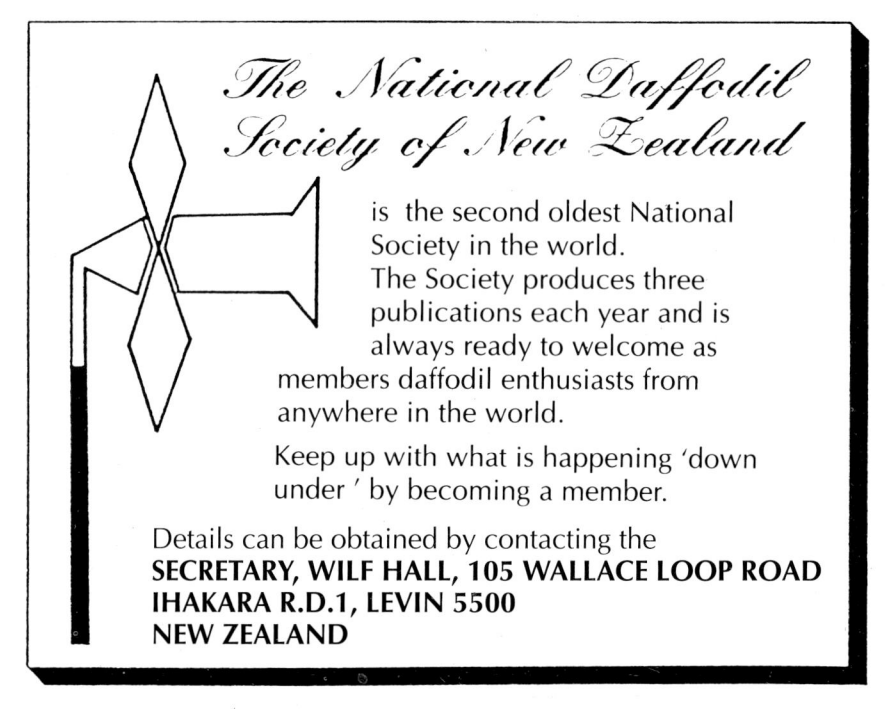

is the second oldest National Society in the world. The Society produces three publications each year and is always ready to welcome as members daffodil enthusiasts from anywhere in the world.

Keep up with what is happening 'down under' by becoming a member.

Details can be obtained by contacting the
**SECRETARY, WILF HALL, 105 WALLACE LOOP ROAD
IHAKARA R.D.1, LEVIN 5500
NEW ZEALAND**

The American Daffodil Society

founded in 1954, invites you to join with over 1400 members around the world to learn the latest cultural information, hints on improving showing technique, and in-depth reports on the newest daffodils. All members receive *The Daffodil Journal*, a 64-page quarterly publication.

Now available: The Illustrated Data Bank, which lists the life histories and descriptions of over 13,000 daffodils, including over 4000 photos. On CD-ROM in either IBM or Macintosh format. $150. Write for computer system requirements.

Memberships are accepted at the rate of $20·00 per year or $50·00 for three years (dollar checks or bank draft, please).

AMERICAN DAFFODIL SOCIETY, INC.
Naomi Liggett, Executive Director
4126 Winfield Rd, Columbus, OH 43220-4606

Index

Authors	Page
Adams, David *N. CYCLAMINEUS* AND ITS HYBRIDS - A SYMPOSIUM	
Tracing Trena Territory in New Zealand	28
Akers, James L MORE AGM DAFFODILS AND TULIPS AGM Tulips	12
BOOK REVIEWS The Tulip	54
RHS TULIP COMPETITION and RESULTS	77
Akers, Wendy A SECOND VISIT TO THE HORTUS BULBORUM	45
OTHER SHOWS City of Belfast Show	87
Bankhead, Delia MINIATURE DAFFODILS FROM DIVISIONS 1 - 4	7
N. CYCLAMINEUS AND ITS HYBRIDS - A SYMPOSIUM	
American Bred Cyclamineus Cultivars	26
The Miniature Cyclamineus Cultivars	30
Blanchard, John *N. CYCLAMINEUS* AND ITS HYBRIDS - A SYMPOSIUM	
Judging Cyclamineus Hybrids	33
DAFFODIL AND TULIP NOTES	
Narcissus × christopheri = N. × koshinomurae	48
Bradbury, Malcolm *N. CYCLAMINEUS* AND ITS HYBRIDS - A SYMPOSIUM	
Breeding Activity and Problems	20
N. cyclamineus in the Wild	22
The English Contribution	23
DAFFODILS AND TULIPS IN LATVIA	38
DAFFODIL AND TULIP NOTES	
The Ralph B White Memorial Medal 1999	50
Daffodils are Poisonous	50
Madam Speaker	52
BOOK REVIEWS AGS Bulb Issue	53
Brandham, Peter NEW CHROMOSOME COUNTS IN NARCISSUS CULTIVARS	39
Dalton, Jan CARLO ALBERTO NAEF - "THE GUV'NOR"	15
Doulton, Janine *N. CYCLAMINEUS* AND ITS HYBRIDS - A SYMPOSIUM	
Division 6 from Ireland	24
Duncan, Brian DAFFODIL AND TULIP NOTES	
The Peter Barr Memorial Cup Awarded to James S Wells	51
Edwards, Alan OTHER SHOWS	
Tulips At Alpine Garden Society Shows	81
Goddard, John RHS EARLY DAFFODIL COMPETITION	65
Grimshaw, John GROWING SNOWDROPS	17
Ingamells, John and Elaine DAFFODIL AND TULIP NOTES What a Delightful Flower	48
James, Tony OVERSEAS SHOWS AND NEWS Pittsburgh Someplace Special	57
Kington, Sally DAFFODIL AND TULIP NOTES	
"Thomas' Virescent Daffodil", syn. The Derwydd Daffodil	47
'White Owl'	52
Leslie, Alan BOOK REVIEWS	
Galanthus Gala 1998	53
SNOWDROPS AT WESTMINSTER	63
Matthews, David MORE AGM DAFFODILS AND TULIPS Wisley Daffodil Trials 1999	11
OTHER SHOWS South East England Daffodil Group Show	85
Nicholl, Reg RHS LATE DAFFODIL COMPETITION	73
Olive, Len RHS DAFFODIL SHOW	67
Pearce, Jim OTHER SHOWS	
The Daffodil Society Show	79
Perrignon, Richard *N. CYCLAMINEUS* AND ITS HYBRIDS - A SYMPOSIUM	
Cyclamineus Hybrids in Australia	30
OVERSEAS SHOWS AND NEWS	
Australian Daffodil Season 1998	58
Skelmersdale, Christine CYCLAMINEUS HYBRIDS IN THE GARDEN	13
Smales, Richard OTHER SHOWS	
Wakefield and North of England Tulip Society	82
Daffodils and Tulips at Harrogate	83
Spotts, Bob DAFFODIL AND TULIP NOTES World Daffodil Council	49
Verge, Frank FOUR DECADES ON	35
Wainwright, John BREEDING ENGLISH FLORISTS' TULIPS	36
Whitsey, Fred OBITUARY; ALAN HARDY VMH	46
Wilkins, Peter RHS EARLY DAFFODIL COMPETITION RESULTS	65
RHS DAFFODIL SHOW RESULTS	69
RHS LATE DAFFODIL COMPETITION RESULTS	74

Daffodil and Tulip Yearbook 1999-2000

Narcissus
Abracadabra 26,30,58
Achduart 85
Aircastle 35
Akepa 43,44
Alacabam 30
Alec Gray 8,9
alpestris 8
Altun Ha 58,83,84,85
Andalusia 24,Fig. 10
Androcles 43
Aosta 25
April Love 86
April Tears 38,44
Arbar 50
Arctic Gold 29
Arish Mell 44,84
Arrival 8
Arrowhead 26
Ashmore 86
Assini 28
assoanus 48
asturiensis 20,23
Atholl Palace 43
Atom 32
Auburn 44
Aurelia 44
aureus 65,Fig.. 2
Ave 35
Baby Moon 44
Baby Star 44
Backchat 29
Badbury Rings 61,68,80,
  84,88
Bagatelle 7,43
Ballykinler 43
Ballynichol 88
Ballyrobert 83
Bandit 60
Bantam 10
Barnesgold 57
Bartley 23,44
Bega 65
Bell Song 44
Bella Donna 58
Belzone 61
Beryl 21,23,44
Bilbo 25
Bird Flight 32
Bird Music 32
Bithynia 67
Blarney 35
Bobbysoxer 44
Bolton 44
Bonny Jean 29
Braid Song 88
Brindle Pink 57
Bryanston 21
bulbocodium 58
bulbocodium subsp. bulbocodium var. conspicuus
  61,84
Bunting 44
Burning Bush 73
Bushtit 44
Buttercup 44
Buttermere Lake 86
Cairntoul 85

California Rose 43
Calleva 58
Camborne 8,9
Cameo Knight 61
Cameo Sun 59,61
Campernelli plenus 84
canaliculatus 61,67
Canasta 38
Candlepower 8,9
Canisp 65
Cantabile 11,74
Cape Cornwall 86
Cape Point 57
Carclew 20,24
Carib 27
Caribbean Snow 80
Castanets 41,42,43
Cathedral Hill 28
Cattistock 24
Cazique 27
Cedric Nice 13
Celestial 44
Centrefold 59,60
Cha-Cha 13
Chanson 88
Chaos 59
Charity May 20,23,24,28,
  44,65
Charles Warren 7
Chaucer 23
Chérie 44
Chesterton 11
Chief Inspector 65
Chobe River 87
Citronita 83
Clare 43,44
Clavier 27
Clouded Yellow 80
Colesbourne 63
Comal 61
Comet 44
Cool Crystal 61,84,85
Cora Ann 44
Coral Light 50
Corky's Song 86
Coromandel 84,86
Cotinga 27,43,44
Cover Girl 60
Crackington 86
Crevette 50,65
Crofty 21,24,Fig. 5
Crowndale 86
Cryptic 60
cuatrecasasii 10
Cupid 32,33
cyclamineus 13-14,20-34,
  58
Cyclone 44
Dailmanach 61,80,85
Dateline 68,73,84,86
David's Gold 60
Dawn Run 57
Daydream 58,80
Debbie Rose 50
Decoy 58
Delia 25
Delta Flight 25,43,44
Delta Wings 25,44

Demand 60
Desert Storm 59
Diatone 43
Dickcissel 44
Dimple 42,43
Dingle Dell 31
Dinkie 10
Dispatch Box 11
Diversity 67
Divertimento 44
Dorchester 43,57,68,74,
  86,88
Douglasbank 7
Dove Wings 23,24,28,44
Dream Prince 58
Drumboe 61
Drumrunie 29
Dunkery 43,86
Dunley Hall 68,83
Durango 28
Eastern Promise 84
Egmont King 60
Eland 44
Elfin Gold 20,25,26
Elizabeth Ann 25,43,44
Elka 8,9,40,43
Elrond 44
Eminent 67
Emperor's Waltz 26
Empress of Ireland 35
Ethelred 61
Ethereal Beauty 57
Ethos 83
Evesham 60,68,85,86
Exit 10
Explosion 41,42,43
Eye Level 43
Eystettensis 10
Fairy Chimes 58,68
Fairy Circle 10
Fairy Footsteps 43
Fairy Glen 43
Fairy Island 73
Fairy King 87
Fairy Wings 44
Falconet 41,42,43
Fanad Head 43
Favor Royal 43
February Gold 14,44
February Silver 44
Ferdie 31,32
fernandesii 48
Ferryman 35
Festivity 35
Filoli 85,87
Finite 27
Fiona MacKillop 35,
  Fig. 12
Fireblade 68
First Born 28
First Kiss 32
First Step 28
Flash Affair 58
Flore Pleno 10
Florence Joy 61
Flute 32
Flyaway 32,33
Flying High 61

Fortune 35
Foundling 13,25,44
Fragrant Rose 83
Freedom Stars 38
Gambas 7,29
Garden Party 50,73, front
  cover
Garden Princess 44
Gay Kybo 74,83,84
Gem of Ulster 50
Georgie Girl 25,43,44
Gimli 44
Gin and Lime 80
Gipsy Queen 8,31
Glacier 35
Glenbrook Mini-Cycla 31,
  32
Glisten 27
Gold Bond 57
Gold Convention 80,85,86
Gold Ingot 87
Golden Amber 87
Golden Aura 84
Golden Cycle 44
Golden Incense 44
Golden Joy 25
Golden Lacquer 44
Golden Perfection 44
Golden Sceptre 44
Golden Strand 87
Golden Vale 59
Golden Years 26
Goldfinger 68,73,80,
  83,84,86,87
Goldhanger 83
Goldmark 59
Grand Prospect 61
Grand Soleil d'Or 42
Greenstar 47
Gresham 43
Gripshover 44
Gulliver 87
Hambledon 74
Hanbury 83
Happy Easter 44
Hartlebury 68
Havelock 35
Hawangi 73
Hawera 28,44
Heamoor 59
Heidi 31
Helford Dawn 65
henriquesii 33
Hero 65
Hesla 65
Highfield Beauty 11,60
Hill Head 43
Hillstar 44
Hollypark 43
Holme Fen 68
Homestead 57,61
Honey Bells 43,44
Honeyorange 57
Hoopoe 41,42,43
Horn of Plenty 44
Hummingbird 13,32
Huon Pride 43
Ibis 27,33

Index

Ice Chimes 44
Ice Follies 38
Ice Wings 43,44,86
Inca 27,33,42,43,44
Innovator 43,50
Interim 25
Interloper 42,43,44
intermedius 67
Intrigue 43,44
Inverpolly 79,80,83
Irish Rose 24
Islander 86
Itzim 26,44,Fig. 6
Jack Snipe 14,44,Fig. 7
Jackadee 57
Jake 57
Jambo 86
Jamestown 43
Jana 44
Jeanette Gower 29
Jenny 13,14,23,24,25, 28,44
Jetage 32
Jetfire 26,26,38,44
Jetsetter 29
Jingle Bells 43,44
Johanna 44
Jonquil Flore Pleno 10
jonquilla 41,43,44
jonquilla stellaris 30
Joybell 23,23,24,25,43, 44
Jumblie 13,41,42
June Lake 57,68,86
Just Joan 35
Kaydee 25
Kehelland 10
Kibitzer 32
Kilmorack 87
Kiltonga 43
Kilworth 50
Kiwi Gossip 60
Kiwi Magic 60,61
Kiwi Solstice 86
Kiwi Sunset 65
Knightsbridge 65
Kokopelli 43,44
Ladies Choice 43,44
Lady Ann 57,68
Lady Diana 58
Lakeland Fair 79,86
Lanarth 44
Lancelot 86
Langley Dandy 58
Lapwing 41,43,44
Larkelly 44
Larkwhistle 44
Last Chance 67,68
Lavender Lass 25
Lemon Heart 44
Lemon Silk 27
Lennymore 86
Liberty Bells 44
Lighthouse Reef 83
Likely Lad 7
Lilac Charm 20,25,40, 43
Lilliput 8

Limbo 57
Limequilla 44
Lincolnshire Double White 43
Lintie 44
Little Beauty 8
Little Becky 33
Little Emma 33
Little Gem 7
Little Miss 32
Little Polly 73
Little Star 32
Little Sunshine 32
Little Witch 14,23,44
Liverpool Festival 74
Loch Alsh 85
Loch Hope 29
Loch Loyal 59,61
Loch Lundie 59
Madam Speaker 52,65, Fig. 25
Magic Moment 86
Magna Vista 28
Mahmoud 35
Mangaweka 29
March Sunshine 44
Marionette 9,42,43,44
Mary Kate 44
Mary Lou 13,25,43,44
Marzo 43
Marzo 44
Matador 41,58
Matika 61
Medici 59
Melbury 43
Mereworth 35
Merrymeet 86
Mickey 31,32
Midas Touch 83
Midget 7,43
Midnight 68
Minicycla 13,23,32,44
Minidaf 7
Minnie 31,32
minor 7
Mission Bells 43,44,68
Misty Glen 84,88
Mite 13,32
Mitylene 23
Mitzy 13,29,31
Mizzen Head 43
Mockingbird 44
Moon Jade 43
Moon Shadow 68,84,86
Moon Tide 43
Moonshine 44
Mortie 31,32,58
Movie Star 67,68
Mt Cook 59
Mulroy Bay 73
Mustardseed 9
My Angel 38,Fig. 15
Naivasha 73
Nanty 31,32
nanus 7
Neahkahnie 86
Neon Light 84
Nether Barr 43,80

nevadensis 30
Newcastle 35
Niade 9
Nice Day 67,68
Nimlet 9
Niveth 44
Nonchalant 88
Northam 9
Norwester 32
Noss Mayo 13,24,Fig. 8
Notre Dame 11,57,73
Nymphette 44
obvallaris 47
Ocean Breeze 27
Ocean Spray 44
odorus 'Campernelli plenus' 84
Opening Bid 32
Orange Glory 44
Orange Queen 44
Oryx 43,44
Osmington 65
Ouzel 27
panizzianus 48
Parcpat 44
Parterre 43
Patabundy 88
Patois 43,84
Paula Cottell 10,67
Peeping Tom 13,14,21,38, 44
Pencrebar 10
Penpol 44
Pequenita 10
Perchance 30
Perfect Spring 26,44
Perky 21,27
Petit Beurre 7
Petrel 79
Phalarope 27
Pheasant's Eye 84
Picarillo 9
Piccolo 7
Picoblanco 9,10
Pink Step 44
Pipers Barn 44
Pipit 44,86
Piraeus 86
Pledge 8
poeticus 21
poeticus recurvus 25
Pol Voulin 88
Polar Morn 60
Polnesk 44
Port Noo 88
Port Patrick 43
Porthchapel 44
Protocol 27
Prototype 43,44
pseudonarcissus 47,48
Purbeck 68,86
Quick Step 44
Quiet Waters 79
Quince 13,41,42
Rainbow 80
Rapture 20,26,29,60, 65,80,84,Fig. 9

Ravenhill 80,84
Red Cameo 61
Red Socks 29
Redlands Too 58
Regal Bliss 87
Reggae 25,43,44
Rikki 67
Ringhaddy 43
Ringleader 84
Ringwood 68
Rip van Winkle 10
Rippling Waters 44
Ristin 29,30
Rival 26
Roberta Watrous 40,43,44
Rockall 84,85
Rockery Gem 8
Rockery White 7,8
Roger 44
Rosaline Murphy 9
Rose Caprice 25
Rose of Tralee 25
Roseworthy 25
Ruby Rose 43
Rufus 29
Rupert 8
rupicola 31,32
rupicola subsp. watieri 10
Samba 44
Sandymount 87
Sassy 30
Satin Blanc 43,44
Satin Doll 84
Saturn Five 29
Savoir Faire 57,73
scaberulus 58
Scarlet Tanager 10
Sealing Wax 65
Segovia 9
Serena Beach 73,80,86
Serena Lodge 11
Sergeant's Caye 80
serotinus 49
Sewanee 9
Sextant 44
Shah 44
Sheer Joy 25,27,43,44
Shining Light 84
Shot Silk 44,86
Shropshire Lass 35
Silent Valley 68,80,86
Silent Valley 80
Silent Valley 86
Silver Bells 40,41,43,44,58
Silver Convention 61
Silver Crystal 73,87
Silver Dream 86
Silverwood 57
Singin' Pub 57
Sir Echo 8
Skater's Waltz 26
Skelmersdale Gold 7
Skylon 44
Slipp'ry 31
Small Talk 7,32
Snipe 13,31
Snook 30,32
Snoopie 44

95

Snow Bunting 44
Snowy Morn 60
Snug 8
Soleil d'Or 42,43
Solveig's Song 86
Soprano 86
Spalding Double White 43
Sparrow 27
Spider 32
Sprite 8,9
Sputnik 25
St Keverne 24,52
Stafford 58
Stanway 84
Star Song 32
State Express 85
Stella Turk 31
Step Child 28
Still Flight 30
Stormy Weather 60
Straight Arrow 26
Stratosphere 57
Strines 80
Sugarbush 44
Sun Disc 43,44,84
Suntrap 73
Sunday Chimes 43,44
Sundial 44
Sunny Maiden 32
Surfside 27
Suzie Dee 20,26,41,43,44
Suzie's Sister 26,41,43,44
Suzy 44
Swagger 31,32
Swallow 27
Swallowcliffe 24
Swedish Fjord 58
Sweet Pepper 44
Sweetness 44
Swift Arrow 13,26
Sydling 44
Tamar Fire 52
Tamar Valley Double White 43
Tanagra 7
Tanya 60
tazetta 41,42
Telamonius Plenus 47
Terrapin 88
Tetherstones 61
Thalia 44
The Alliance 14,20,24,65
Three of Diamonds 10
Tiger Moth 20
Tinkerbell 28
Tiny Tot 7
Titania 24

Tittle-Tattle 44
Toby the First 14
Top Notch 43
Top of the Hill 43
Torr Head 43
Tosca 8
Totten Tot 32
Tracey 13,28,43,44
Trena 13,20,27,28,44,60,65,Fig. 11
Tresamble 44
Trevithian 44
Trigonometry 67
Tripartite 24,84
Triple Crown 74
Trousseau 24
Trudie May 60
Trumpet Warrior 65
Tuesday's Child 44
Tutankhamun 80
Tête-à-Tête 13,41,42
triandrus 58
triandrus subsp. *pallidulus* 58
triandrus subsp. *triandrus* 58
triandrus triandrus 29
Tweeny 9
Twicer 83
Ucluluet Gem 44
Ulster Bank 85
Uncle Duncan 59
Unique 80,83,85
Urchin 44
Utiku 29
Val d'Incles 57,86
Velocity 26
Verdin 44
Verona 86
Verran 58
Vickie Linn 28
viridiflorus 49
Voodoo 30
W P Milner 8,58
Waitetei 60
Warbler 26,65
Warbleton 59
Waterperry 44
Wee Bee 7
Welcome 86
Wheatear 27
Whipcord 43,44
Whitbourne 67
White Caps 27
White Glen 59
White Lady 73
White Owl 52
White Star 84

Wild Rose 25
Willet 60
Wings of Freedom 26
Winter Waltz 27
Woodcock 44
Wren 10
Wyandot 7
× *christopheri* 48
× *koshinomurae* 48
Xit 9,10
Yella-Fella 31
Yellow Prize 44
Yellow Xit 9,10
Yimken 9
Young Blood 88
Zip 32

Galanthus
alpinus 18
Benton Magnet 54
Bill Bishop 64
Blond Inge 63
Cowhouse Green 64
elwesii 18
elwesii 'Joy Cozens' 63
Fenstead End 54
Florence Baker 63
Foxton 54
Hill Poë 64
Joy Cozens 63
koenenianus 54
krasnowii 18
Mighty Atom 63
nivalis 18,63,64
nivalis 'Benton Magnet' 54
nivalis 'Sandersii' 18
peshmenii 54
platyphyllus 18
plicatus 18
Ray Cobb 64
reginae-olgae 18,54
reginae-olgae subsp. *vernalis* 63
Sandersii 18,64
Trym 63

Tulipa
Angélique 12,77
Apeldoorn Elite 85
Apricot Beauty 12
armena 81
aucheriana 81
Avignon 45
Ballerina 45
Barcelona 12,45,Fig. 21
Bessie 37
Black Parrot 82
Blue Bell 12

Canova //
Carnaval de Nice 12
cretica 81
Crystal Beauty 12
Cynthia 12
dasystemon 81
edulis 55
Etude 12
fosteriana 55
Flaming Youth 12
Fringed Beauty 12
Fringed Elegance 12
Friso 12
Gerbrand Kieft 12
Girlfriend 38,Fig. 19
Golden Apeldoorn 85
Golden Oxford 85,Fig. 20
Goldfinder 37
Grand Prestige 12
hageri splendens Fig. 22
Holberg 12
humilis 82
humilis violace 81
James Wild 45
Jaune d'Oeuf 45
julia 81
Kathleen Truxton 45
kurdika 81
Lily Schreyer 12
Maywonder 12
mogoltavica 38
Monte Rosa 12
Music 37
Musical 12
neustruevae 81
Ollioules 12
Olympic Flame 85,Fig. 20
Orange King 45
Orleans 12
Oxford 85
Pink Impression 85,Fig. 20
Prinses Irene 77,Fig. 3
Renown 45
Sevilla 12
schrenkii 81
Sir Joseph Paxton 82
Smyrna 12
sprengeri 53
stapfii 81
Strong Gold 12
suaveolens 81
Synaeda King 5
Ted Turner 12
Tender Beauty 12
Valentine 12
Vivex 12
World Expression 12
vvedenskyi 38